Cecilia Norman ive
cookery. She has ng
since 1969 when s ish
book of recipes fo he
Microwave Cooki in
1980. She concer nd
believes that this ey to success in all types of
cookery. Cecilia is a Fellow of the Institute of Home
Economics and has written many books on various food
topics. Among these, *Barbecue Cookery*, *Pancakes and
Pizzas*, *The Food Processor Cookbook* and her *Microwave Cookery Course* are also available in Grafton Books.

By the same author

Microwave Cookery for the Housewife
The Heartwatcher's Cook Book
The Colour Book of Microwave Cooking
Freezer to Microwave Cookery
The Crepe and Pancake Cookbook (re-titled *Pancake and Pizzas* for paperback)
Microwave Cooking
The Sociable Slimmer's Cookbook
Microwave with Magimix
Microwave Cookery Course
The Pie and Pastry Cook Book
Barbecue Cookery
Sauces, Dressings and Marinades
The Food Processor Cookbook

CECILIA NORMAN'S

Microwave Cookery
For One

GRAFTON BOOKS

A Division of the Collins Publishing Group

LONDON GLASGOW
TORONTO SYDNEY AUCKLAND

Grafton Books
A Division of the Collins Publishing Group
8 Grafton Street, London W1X 3LA

A Grafton Paperback Original 1986

ISBN 0-586-06888-0

Printed and bound in Great Britain by
Collins, Glasgow

Set in Times

Contents

Acknowledgements

I would like to thank my Home Economist Jacqui Belle-fontaine for her help in testing the recipes, which she had to interpret from my scribbled notes; Penny Morris from the Polytechnic of North London who worked with me during her 'vacation'; and Alison Wildman from St Alban's College who assisted during her three-week work-experience period. Only home economists have the patience to try, try and try again, so producing recipes that work. The illustrations are by Eva Stälhammar, a Swedish art student who was staying with me while the book was being prepared. I am confident that this will be the start of a promising career for her.

My thanks go also to the microwave manufacturers for the loan of their microwave ovens for use both in developing recipes and for teaching purposes; to that friendly band of people at Corning and to Michelle Kershaw of Lakeland Plastics who are always interested in new suggestions and ideas; to Alf Howell, my 'solo male' adviser who has cooked for himself for years, and to the several lone ladies from various parts of the country, all of whom have different life-styles.

Lastly, my grateful thanks to my husband Laurie who, though a Chartered Surveyor by profession, transformed himself into a part-time editor and super-nagger to get the manuscript delivered on time, and to Jenny Pouncett who typed it all.

CECILIA NORMAN

Introduction

This book stems from the many letters I have received asking for a microwave cookbook for one. My previous book, *Microwave Cookery Course*, sold lots of copies because I was able to pass on those little tips that are so important in learning how to master cooking by microwave. I hope that this too will be a well-thumbed reference book. Cooking by microwave really does mean that you need never cook by any other means. In practice you will probably still make use of the kettle, the grill, a frying pan and a saucepan or two but, particularly for the single person, the microwave oven is a cooking appliance which enables that person to be as competent in the kitchen as the master cook.

The difficulties of cooking for one are much greater than many people imagine. To start with, shopping can be a problem since you can't always buy in small enough quantities in an economical way. The single person rarely has large storage facilities, particularly when it comes to the refrigerator and the freezer. Some freezers are only suitable for storing already-frozen food and not for actually freezing food down.

To produce a varied menu for one using the conventional cooker, the same number of cooking pots and pans need to be used (albeit of smaller size) as when cooking for a number of people, so there is still as much washing-up in the end.

The single person often finds him- or herself having to resort to rather a monotonous diet and as the statistics indicate that by the end of the 1990s there will be more people living alone than in families, it is about time some attention was given to their needs.

The first thing I had to decide in the preparation of the book was who I was cooking for. Who were all these people living on their own and would they want to cook by microwave? One obvious category was those senior citizens perhaps living a long way from shops, while male or female singles at work all day would constitute the majority. Again, there are some people who will have smallish appetites, whilst others, possibly as a result of their occupation, will require larger portions.

So to compromise, what I have done in this book is to give recipes for a single portion for those with a healthy appetite, but which will suffice for two meals for the person who eats less. Of course you don't want to eat the same thing day after day so any left-overs from one day's main meal will do for a snack for the next day. The microwave is an excellent appliance for reducing the quantity of unwanted food dumped in the dustbin.

While older people tend to cook from scratch, today's liberated person makes use of part-prepared and convenience foods, cooking and reheating for themselves for a variety of work or domestic reasons. This book includes a mixture of both types of prepared foods, bearing in mind the realities of the wide availability of ready-packed prime ingredients.

You can usually buy small quantities of fresh foods and very often small-sized cans and packets, but these latter tend to work out more expensive. But one must bear in mind that although two small cans may cost a few pence more than one large can, if the large one is only partly used and the remaining contents then go bad, it constitutes a loss and not a saving. The same problem applies to frozen foods, unless you are lucky enough to have adequate storage space. If your freezer or freezer compartment is stashed full of large packs of frozen vegetables, then you won't be able to put in any smaller items. One of the main uses of a microwave, as far as a single person is concerned, is that not only can food be cooked but it can also be thawed and reheated. Therefore if you are able to make space in the freezer for a number of smaller items, you can have plenty of variety in your diet.

The freezer is not only designed for stocking frozen uncooked foods; it is also useful for storing freshly cooked servings for future use. With the advent of the microwave and freezer, you are no longer restricted to a monotonous routine. In order to vary your diet further, you could have as many as four fresh vegetables with your everyday chop, burger or chicken pieces. Cook a variety of fresh vegetables at any convenient time and use some of them for that day's meals and freeze or refrigerate the remainder.

But not everyone has a freezer. Even if you haven't, you can still cook in advance or in larger quantities provided you have access to a refrigerator or a cool storage space. Vegetables will keep for a couple of days in a cold larder, but cooked meat must be refrigerated. If you have neither a refrigerator nor a freezer, your back-up to fresh items will have to be canned foods or small quantities of frozen foods to be heated and eaten within a short time of purchase.

When it comes to converting recipes from say a four-person dish to a single portion, a mathematical mind is required for adapting conventional recipes but the microwave recipe cannot be reduced by division. Reducing quantities and timings by a specific percentage doesn't necessarily follow.

It is easier to increase than to decrease a recipe –

basically what you do is to allow between 1½ and 1¾ times the given cooking time when doubling a recipe. Some items when doubled in quantity don't even take as long as this. For example with melted butter it doesn't make much difference how much is being melted. *My advice is to 'look for cooking signs' rather than 'rely on cooking times'.*

Microwave ovens are now available with different dimensions, some being square, others shallow and wide. Sometimes the entire size of the appliance is reduced with the power being equally reduced. If time is not of vital importance to you, then you may be satisfied with the cheaper 500-watt oven. These are about one-third slower than a 700-watt model. Ovens rating 600–650 watts are usually of a similar size to the 700-watt oven which is the highest rating generally of these cookers. I used various types of oven of between 600 and 700 watts output to prepare the recipes given here and the cooking times varied accordingly. Owners of 500-watt-output ovens will almost definitely have to increase the given cooking times by upwards of 10 per cent.

Since cooking times are in direct relation to the quantity of food being cooked, single servings are going to be much quicker both in preparation and length of cooking. A 150 ml (¼ pint) cheese sauce to go with (for example) cauliflower will take only 2 minutes and as you can, if you like, cook and serve in the same dish, the washing-up time too will be minimal.

I haven't included any fancy starters in the book although smaller quantities of some main courses can be utilized and there is a variety of soups.

When you are on your own you may not want to cook splendid meals beautifully garnished every day. My research tells me the important requirement is plain cooking – all-in-one meals and meals of meat, fish or poultry plus plain vegetables are what most people want. In the microwave you can cook old-fashioned stodgy puddings in no time at all and we shouldn't ignore these as they are economical, warming and filling.

Supermarkets are now full of single-portion frozen meals and usually they have microwave-cooking instructions on the packet. I have given charts of cooking methods and times for a selection of these frozen foods.

The book has been devised to include slow, medium and fast recipes – but one must confess that even the slowest ones are pretty speedy by conventional cooking standards.

The Basics of Microwave Cookery

When you take delivery of your new microwave, have a good look at the box where you will usually find instructions for unpacking it. It is a good idea to keep all the packaging in case you have to return the machine for any reason, or transport it to another home.

Remove all the wrappings including any adhering plastic and attach a 13-amp three-pin plug fitted with a 13-amp fuse. (Some plugs only contain a 3-amp fuse.) Remove any books and packages that may have been placed inside the cabinet.

Having sited your microwave oven and plugged it into the chosen electric point, put a jug or glass of water on the oven shelf or turntable and close the door. Open the instruction book that came with the oven and go through all the processes. At this stage you will certainly not memorize them all, but if you can just perfect the operation of the timer and power controls, you will be able to start to cook. The placing of a jug or glass of water in the oven cavity will prevent any damage to the magnetron which might occur if the appliance were inadvertantly switched on with nothing in the oven.

Provided that you choose your menus with an eye to what the microwave is good at, you should be successful every time. But before you can reach the dizzy heights of a microwave cordon bleu, a number of techniques must be mastered. It is also a very great help to understand microwave cooking patterns and the factors which influence the cooking results and cooking times.

Microwave cooking is different from conventional

methods and although many of the ways of doing things are similar – for example, stirring – the reasons for doing these may not be so. Do not be misled into thinking that microwaves can imitate old-fashioned methods. They cannot and should not. However, most microwave-prepared food, particularly if thoughtfully selected, is superior. This is because of the rapid speed of cooking and the need for less liquid.

Microwaves cook by one system alone – by vibrating the tiny particles in the food, which then become hot by friction. In conventional methods, food is either cooked by means of hot air or by radiant heat, which either heats a liquid which then cooks the food (e.g. in boiling and steaming) or acts directly on the food item, for example a joint, jacket potato or cake (i.e. in roasting, baking or grilling). In conventional deep frying the fat is heated first and then cooks the food by conduction, while shallow-fried food is cooked by action of the heat on both the fat and the food. It is very important to note that deep frying in the microwave is proscribed as the temperature of the fat cannot be controlled, so it is no good considering fritters and battered items.

With the microwave, contact frying in a tablespoon of fat or oil, using a special browning dish (which itself becomes very hot) means that you can sear, seal, brown and lightly fry, amongst other things, burgers, sausages, bacon and crumb-coated fish.

Gentle sautéeing in butter of vegetables, such as chopped onions, is most acceptable but it must be noted that the microwaves are heating both the fat and the vegetables at the same time. Browning signifies the beginning of burning and this is not just restricted to the outside of the food, but it works very well as far as flavour is concerned. Sautéed potatoes are not possible because no crisp surface occurs but 'sweating', a recognized culinary term, in which the sautéeing is carried out with a certain amount of steam to develop the flavour, produces excellent results.

Some foods normally baked or roasted in the conventional way can also be recommended for cooking by microwave – chicken, mincemeat loaf and jacket potatoes for example. Most foods normally boiled or steamed will cook better by microwave, and these include vegetables and fish.

Unless you are restricted to cooking by microwave alone you are likely to have other cooking means and you will want to use the conventional oven, the grill and the frying pan from time to time and the kettle probably frequently. The pressure cooker also has its own special uses as does the slow cooker, and these cannot be replaced by the microwave.

However, taken over all, any meal can be cooked all or mostly by microwave. A good example of a microwave-cooked menu would be:

> Cream of Mushroom Soup
> Baked Whole Plaice
> Courgettes
> Carrots
> Jacket Potatoes
> Ginger Pudding

The microwave oven can cope admirably with the lot.

On the other hand an *unsuitable* choice of meal for the microwave would be:

> Crispy Deep Fried Battered Fish
> Chips
> Hot Lemon Soufflé

However, if you would be satisfied with crumbed fish and oven chips, you could cook both – admittedly they would not be as crisp but they also would not be as fattening, having been cooked in practically no fat and absorbing only a fraction of that. The soufflé *could* be microwaved but would not have a browned crispy top.

Most menus can be cooked partly by microwave and partly by the old-fashioned methods. Let us consider a Sunday lunch, which you may be unlikely to cook just for yourself:

> Roast beef
> Yorkshire pudding
> Roast potatoes
> Sprouts
> Roast parsnips
> Apple pie

If the joint is small, this can be cooked completely or partially by microwave. The Yorkshire pudding *must* be cooked in a hot conventional oven. To roast the potatoes, first cook them in a covered dish containing two table-spoons of salted water; drain and complete the cooking in a dish of hot fat in the conventional oven. The sprouts can be cooked entirely by microwave. The roast parsnips are cooked in the same way as the potatoes. As to the apple pie, the fruit can first be cooked in the microwave, then after the pastry lid is put on the whole pie can be finished in the hot oven.

I am quite sure that a menu doesn't exist where the microwave can't help in some way.

Microwave cooking times are governed by the amount of food you are cooking. Conventional cooking times may vary for some cookery but not for others, e.g. an hour is needed to cook either one or forty jacket potatoes in the conventional oven. The same amount of time is needed to boil either one pound or two pounds of potatoes. A sponge cake will take thirty-five to forty minutes to bake but a hundred fairy cakes will take only fifteen minutes. In other words it is the mass of each item of food which determines timings conventionally.

In the microwave there are many influencing factors which govern the cooking time. Success depends not only on correct timing, but on the depth of the food in the dishes, the type of food that you are cooking, the strength of the power setting (e.g. Full, Medium, Defrost). Once you have got used to your oven and discovered for yourself the best timings and most suitable containers, your problems will be over. No author can know what your precise needs are in your own kitchen.

Timings cannot be exact for any one of the following reasons:

1. The wattage of your oven may be rated anything between 500 and 700 watts.
2. A 10 per cent tolerance is admitted by manufacturers – thus a 600-watt oven may be operating on 540 (minus 10 per cent) or 660 (plus 10 per cent).
3. Line and voltage vary from day to day.
4. The containers used – their shape and what they are made of.
5. The starting temperature of the food – whether taken direct from the freezer, the refrigerator, the cold larder or at room temperature.
6. The volume of food being cooked: in microwaving, it is the amount that counts – in conventional cooking, the amount will not make much difference.
7. If another electrical appliance is plugged in to the same circuit and operated simultaneously.

Although you can get three or four small dishes of different foods in the microwave oven at the same time, their cooking or reheating will not all take the same time.

Different foods heat at different rates so that you will have to inspect frequently to see which of the dishes needs to be removed. The advantage of cooking in volume, and the reduction in microwave cooking time that results from that volume, is cancelled out by the time you waste opening and closing the door. It is far better to microwave one dish at a time, in descending order of length of cooking time.

The best way to cook in any medium is to recognize the various stages, noting when a cake mixture becomes dry on top or a thickening occurs around the edges of a sauce. Use the timings given in any microwave recipe as a guide only and initially give 30 seconds or so less, adding any necessary extra time until the food is cooked. You will soon get used to your own microwave. If you find that timings from several recipes taken from any particular source are too short, you can be pretty sure that you will have to add more time to all of them.

Microwaves work by causing friction between the molecules of the food, creating greater and greater heat – the process being the same whether defrosting, cooking or reheating. There is a greater concentration of heat around the edges because the microwaves are entering both from the top and the sides so that the edges receive much more microwave attention. Occasional stirring will help to equalize the heat throughout the food item being microwaved.

Jugs, bowls or dishes should be compact enough to contain the food throughout the microwaving process, taking into account that food frozen in blocks will spread out when thawed. A narrow container is adequate if it does not become still narrower towards the top. Actually, narrow shapes are preferable because as the width is less than in a short wide container, less frequent stirring is necessary.

Covering, used in conventional cooking to keep in the heat and reduce evaporation, is equally necessary in microwaving. Vented cling film, non-stick paper, suitable casserole or purpose-designed lids for microwave use are needed. I find that greaseproof paper tends to stick to the food so I have stopped using it, although it is perfectly safe to use in the microwave. Because of the build-up of heat and the resulting steam, tightly lidded containers should not be used for either cooking or reheating.

When cooking in a roasting bag or boilable bag, remember to leave a small gap at the top for steam to escape. You can use special plastic seals or elastic bands. When cooking plastic-pouched 'ready to eat meals', place in a dish and slash or pierce the top of the bag before microwaving, otherwise it may burst. Ordinary polythene or sandwich bags are not suitable for microwave cooking, as they cannot support the weight of the hot contents.

Boiling over is a problem which is overcome in the microwave by venting. Cling film covering should be released at one of the corners, leaving a small gap to vent. Lids on dishes containing a large volume of starchy or syrupy liquids, unless they have a hole in them, should be balanced or wedged open with a wooden cocktail stick. It is easy to wipe any spillage from the microwave, but if you are cooking something that persistently boils over, then reduce the setting in exactly the same way as you turn down the gas or electricity on the conventional hob. If you do not have a choice of setting, a larger and taller container should be used and give the cooking frequent short rests. As a rule less liquid is used in microwave cooking, which in itself lessens the likelihood of boil-overs.

Hotspots. Turning is not always necessary and stirrable foods never need turning. In every microwave, no matter how full of refinements, there will be some hotter areas – that means those where the microwaves bunch together and so work harder and create more friction. Manufacturers strive hard to overcome these hot spots by introducing various methods of dispensing the microwaves. These include turntables, stirrers and antennae.

It is true to say that there are also hotter areas in any conventional oven. This can sometimes be at the sides and sometimes at the back. Unless you have a conventional oven in which hot air circulation is aided by a fan, food will be cooked and browned more quickly at the top than at the bottom of the oven.

Once having discovered which parts of your conventional oven or your microwave are hotter, you can place your dishes strategically in either. There are various ways of detecting where the hot spots are in a microwave. In an oven without a turntable, I would suggest that each time you make a cup of coffee you put the cup in a different place and time how long it takes to heat. With a turntable, set the cup at different distances from the outside edge and again time the heating process. In no time at all the hot spot will be detected, and this will never change its position. Once discovered always put the narrow-diametered vessels at this point for greatest speed.

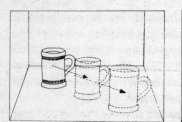 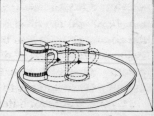

Larger dishes will inevitably cover both hot and cold spots. To overcome this, all you have to do is reposition or turn the dish occasionally during cooking. The problems are minimized when cooking for one since the dishes and containers employed will be smaller. In any case, you will be able to see if one side is cooking more quickly and then, if necessary, give it a half turn or push the dish forwards or backwards.

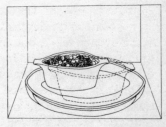

Turning over, when using your microwave oven, mainly applies when using the browning dish, or when using an ordinary dish an even coating of oil or sauce is desirable. Turning over is also necessary when cooking items more than an inch thick, as the microwaves penetrate in such a strange fashion. A jacket potato or baked apple is likely to cook unevenly, not only because of its shape, but also because of the moisture content. What happens is that microwaves coming from the top cook the most strongly and although the underside receives less microwave activity, the heat created (because the potato is full of moisture) causes steam to build up in the lower part of the potato where it gets trapped against the base plate. It cannot evaporate as it does from the remainder of the potato's surface and so the bottom heats very quickly indeed. Hence it needs to be turned.

Stirring. Where food items are covered during cooking,

stirring is facilitated if only three-quarters of the bowl or dish are covered with cling film. You can then easily insert the spoon without having to reposition the covering.

Repositioning of food is necessary when more than one item is being cooked simultaneously. Two chops cooking in a dish may have to be turned over or moved if one is cooking more quickly than the other.

Shielding is sometimes required when cooking unevenly shaped food. The thinner parts will obviously cook fastest. In particular bones easily absorb microwave heat, causing the flesh attached to them to cook too rapidly. To protect those parts they can be wrapped in small pieces of smooth cooking foil. *The foil must not touch the sides of the oven cabinet.* Since the microwaves cannot penetrate the foil, the covered sections can only be gently cooked by conduction of heat from the exposed parts of the food item.

Some manufacturers discourage the use of any type of metal. It is therefore essential that you follow their instructions, as they cannot be held responsible for any damage that may occur if you do use metal. I can only say that I have had no problems on this score.

Drying out. Some items of food, such as slices of reheated meat, tend to dry out during reheating. If they are shielded by either a spoonful of sauce or covered with a layer of potato, they will remain moist.

Standing times – this is probably the most difficult microwave-cooking term to understand. It simply means that, exactly as in conventional cooking, heat spreads through the food after it is taken from the heat source and the current is switched off. A joint roasted conventionally should never be carved immediately, otherwise juices seep out rather than settling throughout the meat. It is just the same when a joint is cooked by microwave. The difference lies in the fact that in conventional baking, the food is cooked entirely by conduction of one hot layer against the next, whilst in microwave cooking this conduction only commences after the first inch or so is hot. Because of this the thick outer band of food retains an even greater heat and would be well and truly overdone if microwaving were continued until the inside was completely cooked. During the standing time the inside will catch up to maintain an even temperature throughout the joint. After cooking, cover loosely with foil to hold in the heat.

Thin items, such as chicken breasts or fish fillets, need practically no standing time. Open-textured cakes and puddings must have a standing time before being turned out. If they are over-cooked they will become doubly so, and resemble solid rocks after the standing time. When cooking on the Defrost setting no standing time will be required.

Popping. Any items covered with a skin will pop or burst during microwaving, so that liver, kidney, apples, peppers, etc. must be pricked, scored or cut to release the pressure which would otherwise build up inside. A prime example of the dangers of cooking enclosed ingredients whole are eggs – you must never, ever, try to cook an unshelled egg directly in the microwave. It will burst in a mini-explosion, covering the oven in tiny fragments which will take ages to clean off. Shelled raw eggs, unless carefully treated and cooked, covered, on a low setting, will also burst as the yolk is covered in a thin membrane. Whole shelled hard-boiled eggs must not be reheated or the same thing may happen.

Chicken sinews and bones in fish can cause popping, and it can occur with fish cooked in their skins. It is a good idea to cover these foods with non-stick paper or cling film and leave this in position for a moment or two after taking the dish from the microwave oven.

Defrosting and reheating. Basic defrosting methods depend very much on the food you are trying to defrost and you will find information and directions in Chapter 4. Reheating should be treated in the same way as cooking – covering these foods that need to be kept moist with vented cling film, an upturned plate or lid, or using non-stick paper on those that you wish to keep crisp.

When heating a plate of mixed items push them as near to the centre of the plate as possible. Make a depression in the centre of mashed potato mounds, and form peas, cut beans, sweetcorn kernels and the like into a pyramid. Cover sliced meat with gravy or add a tea-spoon of water.

A meal on a plate will take about 2 minutes to reheat. Pasta heats more slowly and is best when mixed in with the sauce. Puddings and pudding portions take about 30 seconds and can be reheated uncovered but take care where there is syrup or jam, which becomes very hot very quickly.

As a guideline, you can take it that any food which takes a short time to cook will take a correspondingly brief period to reheat. Foods which take a long time to cook will take a longer time to reheat. Generally, you need to allow about a quarter to one half the original cooking time.

When uncertain about the timing for reheating plates of mixed items, set the oven on half power or on the Defrost (30 per cent) setting. It will take a little longer but all the food items will be equally hot.

A good way to test for the temperature of reheated food is to feel the underneath of the plate. Alternatively, if cling film has been used as a cover, it is possible to feel the surface of the food through it.

Foods requiring particular care when cooking (such as baked custards, which must be cooked on a Low setting) must be reheated on the same setting and those that are stirrable, should be stirred once during reheating and once again before serving.

Now that you have read and digested the introductory chapters and had a good look at your manufacturer's guide book, you should be in a position to go ahead with your microwaving with every confidence.

Utensils and Containers

Have a look in the cupboard before embarking on a shopping trip to buy special crockery and utensils. You may well find that you have plenty of suitable dishes to be going on with like mixing bowls, glass dishes and casseroles and stoneware.

If you live on your own, it won't matter if you don't have a full set of matching items – so long as those you do have are suitable for microwave use. Both the materials that the dishes or bowls are made of and also their shape and size are vital factors here. Cookware must be made of materials that allow the free passage of the microwaves into the food without the microwaves having any effect on the containers themselves. Anything containing or decorated with metal, including gold or silver inscriptions, must not be used in the microwave oven. Foil is acceptable only in certain circumstances which are explained later in this chapter.

Glassware Clear ovenglass such as Pyrex is a good choice, particularly as you can very often mix, cook and serve from the same container. This type of glass can resist very high cooking temperatures although it cannot be used over direct heat or close to a hot grill.

Coloured or decorated ovenglass except when trimmed (as stated above) with gold or silver, is almost as good except that cooking may be marginally slower.

Cheap tumblers and wine glasses, dessert dishes and bowls are fine for heating, but are not recommended for lengthy cooking as the heat of the contents may cause the glass to crack. No milk bottles please – the narrow neck stops the steam from escaping and the liquid would erupt.

You may find that you have an inexpensive glass salad bowl in good condition that could do a turn in the microwave but you must be absolutely sure that the glassware contains no invisible metal. An example of this is crystal which contains lead. Never, never put crystal in the microwave, as it will undoubtedly explode – particularly *after* it has been removed from the microwave.

Glass ceramics on the other hand are both strong and suitable. Corning ware (not to be confused with microwave-proof white porcelain dishes such as flan dishes with recipes printed on their base) can also be used in the freezer, on the hob, in the conventional oven and under the grill. The only time these would break would be if dropped or if used when a crack has developed.

Pottery and stoneware These items (not iron stoneware) are eminently suitable and they can look very attractive which increases their acceptability for oven-to-table use. To make absolutely sure that your casseroles and dishes are going to be safe, put just one of the set into the microwave oven together with a jug containing 150 ml (¼ pint) cold water. Switch on at Full Power for 1 minute, then feel the temperature of the dish and also the water. If the water is hotter than the dish, then that dish and all of that range will be satisfactory for use in the microwave. If the dish is warm, then it can be used for short although frequent cooking periods; if the dish feels hotter than the water in the jug you can be sure that there is some metal content or impurity which after a time would cause breakage. Damaged or cracked dishes are likely to break because the microwaves will cause greater heating on the soiling in the crack causing it to open up.

China can be used safely for microwave purposes but it again must have no metal (such as gold or silver decoration). Antique china is not recommended just in case it crazes and you find you have destroyed a valuable piece. Cups of coffee, cocoa etc can be heated and reheated in the microwave oven, but you must make sure that the handles are all in one with the cup and not just glued on. The glue may well melt and you can imagine the problems caused when grasping the drooping handle of a hot cup of liquid.

You can actually boil water in the teapot in the microwave but it might take fractionally longer than water boiled in the kettle.

Plastic ware Plastic boxes, dishes and trays abound. As long as you are aware of the pros and cons you will find certain of them both cheap and useful. The main point to consider is what you are going to use them for – ordinary plastics cannot resist very high temperatures so that they are not suitable for *any* method of cooking. However, ranges of plastic cookware are being specifically designed for either microwave or conventional and microwave use. Some have a longer life expectancy than others. At the bottom of the range are the dishes made of polyethylene, which are recognizable by touch, as they are *not* rigid. These cannot be used in the conventional oven or under the grill and will distort in the microwave if used for cooking items such as bacon, sausages or chops or for making puddings with syrup or jam underneath. I like ramekin dishes, pudding basins and ring moulds. The only drawback is you generally have to buy a pack of five. However it is possible to obtain by mail order a pack of mixed shapes.

If you have only a small freezer or freezer compartment, rectangular single-portion dishes and divided trays which will accommodate a meal containing, for example, meat and two vegetables, are useful as they can be stacked economically so leaving space for other things.

Continuous usage (i.e. long-life) containers are quite expensive but can be used for all kinds of microwave cooking.

Thermoplastics are part of the family of plastic materials that can be used in both conventional and microwave ovens. They can resist temperatures up to 200°C (400°F). Yogurt pots are unsuitable because they cannot withstand boiling liquids although, strangely enough, some soured cream pots (which are slightly softer to the touch) are good for heating the odd drop of milk. Polystyrene foam dishes, apart from being incapable of resisting fats or (when tightly covered) trapped-in steam, are also insulated so that defrosting on one of these supermarket-type trays takes longer. Ordinary polythene bags are not suitable but roasting bags, boil-in bags and cling film can all be used, but you must not use the metal tags. Plastic boxes without their lids can be used for the initial defrosting of food, as they will not become affected until the foods themselves become hot.

Paper Paper plates, greaseproof paper, baking parchment and kitchen paper all have their microwave uses, either to reheat on, to cover, or to absorb excess moisture or fat. Don't use waxed plates or dishes because the wax will melt. Also don't put the decorated side of kitchen paper against the food and don't leave paper items alone in the microwave for they will burn. Do not line the base of the oven with any of these materials – the microwave oven needs no protection as spillage is so easy to wipe up. Never use recycled paper because it may have some metallic content.

Ovenable board is a type of polyester-coated paper which is made into dishes and plates. The dishes are meant to be disposable and can be used in the conventional as well as the microwave oven.

Metal and why you can't use it There are two types of metal – the dense and the flimsy. Among the dense are casseroles made of iron with a vitreous enamel finish that are often used in conventional cookery. You could be forgiven for mistaking these for ordinary pottery as sometimes they are brightly coloured. Microwaves cannot pass through these so that the food inside will not even become warm let alone cook.

Flimsy metals include tags for fastening, roasting or ordinary polythene bags, butter papers, chocolate wrappings, decoration on plates and cups. These are all dangerous because 'short circuiting' occurs as the metal reflects the microwaves back to the magnetron.

If metal touches the sides of the microwave oven it will cause pitting of the walls, which subsequently spoils the 'pattern' of the microwaves as they bounce about the cavity.

Flashing and crackling will immediately alert you if an unsuitable metallic object has been placed in the cavity by mistake. You should switch off the oven immediately. Continual 'arcing' can cause paper around metal tags to catch fire; fortunately this will be enclosed in the cabinet which limits the amount of air available to fan any flames.

Frozen ready-to-heat meals are now being packaged in plastics, but when buying these in foil dishes follow the basic rules on page 35.

You can if you wish safely re-use any of these foil

dishes that are no more than 1cm (¾ in) in depth if they are filled to the brim with food and provided the metal is not in contact with the sides of the microwave and the manufacturers of your oven do not proscribe such use. Should you decide to heat two such containers side by side, make certain either (a) that they are more than 2.5 cm (1 in) apart or (b) that adjoining sides of the dishes are literally touching each other. Any *small* space between would create arcing.

It is essential to follow the directions given in your microwave oven guide book because manufacturers do vary in their requirements about metal, and with the new generation of combination ovens the rules are slightly different.

Container shapes Strange as it may seem, not only the type of material but also the shape of a container, influences cooking times. The narrower the diameter of your container, the more successful you will be with your microwave cookery and it is here that the single person scores because he or she has no need for very large cooking containers.

Round and oval shapes are better than square or rectangular because there are no sharp corners where overcooking can occur. Choose shallow rather than very tall dishes because high sides may slightly slow the cooking times and it is also difficult to stir foods in a tall pot without first removing it from the oven. Ring-shaped moulds are good for cakes and meat loaves because cooking takes place more rapidly in a circular shape, and as the centre is a void there is no food in the area where cooking is slowest. Narrow jugs have a shorter diameter so that the food is evenly cooked while bowls are especially good as their rounded bases allow for even mixing and stirring.

Containers must be tall enough to allow for liquids to boil up without actually boiling over, and cakes and puddings to rise without spilling over.

Choice of cookware When cooking by microwave you can in fact use all sorts of containers not necessarily designed for culinary use. Plant pots or cardboard boxes lined with non-stick paper or cling film are all useful. (You can buy non-stick paper known as Bakewell parchment from most stationers or from Lakeland Plastics or similar mail order firms.)

I have confined my choice of dishes in this book to bowls of various sizes, small casseroles (because it is often more convenient to cover with a lid than with cling film) and glass measuring jugs. Here is a list of some items that I used in creating the recipes:

> 1 litre (1¾ pint) squat shape glass
>   measuring jug
> 0.55 litre (1 pint) glass measuring jug
> 0.75 litre (1¼ pint) round casserole
> 1.25 litre (2¼ pint) round casserole
> 0.4 litre (¾ pint) oval pie dish or server
> 0.75 litre (1¼ pint) oval pie dish
> 21.5 cm (8½ in) round pie dish
> 0.75 litre (1¼ pint) loaf dish
>   (19 × 10 × 5 cm (7½ × 4 × 2 in))
> 2 × 200 ml (7 fl oz) glass ramekin dishes
> 0.55 litre (1 pint) bowl
> 1 litre (1¾ pint) bowl
> 1.95 litre (3½ pint) bowl
> Browning dish with lid
> Wire whisk
> Cling film
> Plastic vented lid

One of the problems with microwaved food is that because the dishes are heated only by conduction from the food, they don't seem to have the ability to keep the food as hot as a dish taken straight from a conventional oven. The smaller the quantity of food, the shorter the cooling-down period will be so it is advisable to commence your meal as soon as the food is ready. (However, you will nearly always need to use oven gloves to remove the plates and dishes from the microwave oven.)

But there are some cooking dishes which themselves become very hot because they actually absorb the microwaves – amongst these is the Pyrex Vision range. The material is very tough (it is used for the undersides of spacecraft) and will not break in microwave use. The considerable advantage of these dishes is that because they themselves become hot, the food correspondingly stays hot for some time.

Browning dishes Browning dishes are a valuable addition and not a gimmick for microwave-oven owners. They come in different shapes and sometimes have lids. When the empty and unlidded dish is put in the microwave and the oven is switched on at Full Power, the microwaves heat the base of the dish because it is coated with a substance that attracts the microwaves. The remainder of the dish will remain cool.

When you purchase a browning dish, you will find a leaflet with the manufacturers' recommended pre-heating times in the box – the maximum must never be exceeded. Should you wish to cook a second item immediately after the first, you will need to give the empty, albeit soiled, dish a few seconds' booster. Ceramic or glass base plates, shelves or turntables, naturally become hot during the pre-heating and cooking process so it is inadvisable to reheat the browning dish repeatedly at any one time.

Some ovens have a metal base or turntable plate which, although more resistant to the heat of the browning dish, may retard its heating propensity. (Some manufacturers supply or recommend a special protective mat which is placed underneath the browning dish.)

To obtain the maximum browning, it is best to start with the food at room temperature. Obviously, it is not always possible to do this, particularly if the food is stored at a lower temperature for health and hygiene reasons – it is never a good idea to leave meat, fish or poultry in a warm atmosphere before cooking. An easy method is to pop the food into the microwave and set on Defrost or Full Power for a few seconds to take the chill off, then pre-heat the browning dish.

Immediately the dish is hot enough and without removing it from the microwave oven, press the food against the surface and continue cooking as required. (Of course you cannot press eggs!) If your browning dish has a lid the whole can be used as a casserole so that, after browning the meat etc, other ingredients together with the liquid can be added. Place the lid in position and continue cooking.

Browning dishes become very hot, reaching a temperature of 300°C (600°F), and so must never be put directly on to a work surface or cloth. Oven gloves will be needed for all types, except the small 'menuette' which has a handle.

Microwave-cooking Charts

It is not uncommon for lone eaters to read a newspaper, magazine or book while enjoying their meal. I am hoping that you will spend such moments browsing through this book where you will find, not only recipes, but general cooking instructions.

Charts are always useful for easy reference and this section includes a guide to heating liquids to give you an idea of how long your cup of coffee will take to heat as well as timings for defrosting and heating convenience foods.

We all resort to buying convenience foods from time to time. Frozen dishes are probably the most popular but canned and packeted foods are also easy to store. Manufacturers are now including microwave instructions on many of their products.

Aluminium foil containers Items frozen in foil dishes and packed in cardboard cartons can be heated in the microwave if you follow the instructions recommended by the Aluminium Foil Container Manufacturers Association.

Step 1: Remove the aluminium foil container from the carton. If it contains a frozen food product there is no need to defrost.

Step 2: Remove the lid (foil, plastic or foil-laminated board) from the aluminium foil container.

Step 3: Return the aluminium foil container to the original carton, leaving one end partially open.

Step 4: Place the carton in the microwave oven and heat. (the carton eliminates any risk of arcing). Because the aluminium foil reflects microwaves the heating of the food takes place through the top only, leading to more even heating over a slightly longer period. Steam generated inside the carton helps the food cook more completely and evenly. Pies cooked in foil containers come out of the oven with an appetizing crust, the foil container remaining firm and easy to handle despite the moist, hot pie-filling inside.

And a bonus! Any spillage resulting from liquid boiling over the edge of the container will be held within the carton rather than soiling the oven.

Step 5: After speedy microwave cooking the meal can be brought to the table in its own sturdy, aluminium serving dish.

Plastic containers Foods frozen in plastic dishes may usually be thawed without turning out, but you may prefer to transfer the frozen food and reheat it on the serving plate and then you will have no need to warm the plate.

Some frozen meals come in boil-in-the-bag pouches and these require slightly different treatment – the following chart gives details. If in a foil dish follow the instructions for foil dishes on page 35 or otherwise transfer to a plate or dish.

Thawing and Heating Some Convenience Foods

Items	Instructions
Roast Beef in Gravy	Cover loosely and heat on Full Power for 3–4 minutes. Stand 2 minutes before serving.
Meat Balls in Sauce	Put in dish, cover loosely with lid or cling film, heat on Full Power for 6–7 minutes, stirring once during cooking.
Meat Pies (individual)	Wrap in kitchen paper and heat on Defrost (30 per cent) for 10 minutes.
Shepherd's Pie	Cover with greaseproof paper, heat on Defrost (30 per cent) for 10–15 minutes and brown under the grill.
Steak and Kidney Pudding (individual)	Transfer to small bowl or casserole, cover loosely with cling film or lid and heat on Defrost (30 per cent) for 10–15 minutes.
Boil-in-the-Bag Foods (individual)	Slit the bag; put, slit-side up, in dish, heat on Defrost (30 per cent) for 5 minutes, flex the bag, then heat on Full Power for 2–3 minutes.
Casseroles or Stewed Meats in Sauce	Cover loosely and heat on Full Power for 5–7 minutes, stirring occasionally.
Chicken or Duck à l'Orange	Put pouch in dish, slit top, heat on Full Power for 6 minutes.
Smoked Haddock with Butter	Put pouch on plate, slit top of pouch, heat on Full Power for 5–7 minutes.
TV Dinner	Follow directions regarding foil containers (page 35) and heat on Full Power for 6–7 minutes and stand for 1–2 minutes.
Macaroni Cheese	Cover loosely with cling film or lid, heat on Full Power for 6–7 minutes, stirring once during heating.
Lasagne	Cover loosely with cling film or lid, heat on Defrost (30 per cent) for 10–15 minutes.
Stuffed Cannelloni in Sauce	Put in dish, cover loosely with cling film or lid and heat on Defrost (30 per cent) for 10–15 minutes.
Mince Pie (individual pre-baked)	Wrap in kitchen paper, put on plate and heat on Full Power for 30 seconds.
Fruit Pie (individual pre-baked)	Put on kitchen paper and heat on Defrost (30 per cent) for 5 minutes.

Thawing and Heating Some Convenience Foods (cont.)

Items	Instructions
Bread Roll from frozen	Wrap in kitchen paper, heat on Full Power for 10–20 seconds.
Small loaf	Wrap in kitchen paper and thaw on Defrost (30 per cent) for 4 to 6 minutes.
Cakes, small	Put on kitchen paper and thaw on Defrost for 10–20 seconds.
Gâteau, 1 slice	Put on kitchen paper and thaw on Defrost (30 per cent) for 15–20 seconds.
Mousse	Thaw in package on Defrost (30 per cent) for 10–20 seconds.
Trifle	Remove from wrapping, put on serving plate and thaw uncovered on Defrost (30 per cent) for 30–45 seconds.

Heating Liquids (on full Power)

Item	Amount	Time
Water	150 ml (¼ pint)	1¾ minutes to boiling
	200 ml (⅓ pint)	2¼ minutes to boiling
	300 ml (½ pint)	3¼ minutes to boiling
	600 ml (1 pint)	6 minutes to boiling
Coffee (black)	1 cup	1¾ minutes to hot
Milk	150 ml (¼ pint)	1½ minutes to boiling
	300 ml (½ pint)	2½ minutes to boiling
	600 ml (1 pint)	4 minutes to boiling

Tablespoon equivalents

2 heaped tablespoons quick macaroni equals 50 g (2 oz)
3 level tablespoons grated cheese equals 25 g (1 oz)
5½ level tablespoons fresh breadcrumbs equals 25 g (1 oz)
4 level tablespoons lentils equals 50 g (2 oz)
4 level tablespoons long-grain rice equals 50 g (2 oz)

————————*SOME AFTERTHOUGHTS*————————

Cooked pastry items do not become crisp when thawed and reheated by microwave, neither will rolls and breads have an extra-crispy crust. When cooking from raw, Shortcrust Pastry is pallid, but wholemeal is acceptable. Suet pastry is much more successful (whether freshly cooked or reheated) and canned steak and kidney pudding is excellent, although the canned steak and kidney pie comes out soft.

To reheat tinned steak and kidney pudding, remove from the can and put, round side up, on a dish. Cover with vented cling film and heat on Full Power for 2–3 minutes.

With tinned sponge pudding, remove from the can and place the pudding, topping side uppermost, on a plate. Heat, without covering, on Full Power for about 2 minutes. To reheat one portion, allow only about 30 seconds.

To reheat a single portion of home-made beef casserole, place it in a small dish and heat, covered, for 1 minute.

Soups

A soup can be used as a starter or as a main meal. Home-made soups are so easy to make by microwave that you may choose to rely on cans and packets only in emergency. Perhaps an advantage of the can or packet is that it is easy to store, but if you have a freezer compartment – no matter how small – you can always find room for a half pint of soup. A good way to prepare soup for freezing is to make it very concentrated – either by using less liquid in the recipe, or by longer cooking so that more is evaporated. Add extra boiling water from the kettle before thawing or after reheating.

It is easy to open a can when in a hurry, but the soup must be emptied into a bowl for microwaving. Reheating takes about 3 minutes but the process is a little quicker if the bowl is partially covered. However thick soups tend to boil over so the bowl should only be half filled. Thick soup takes longer than thin and whichever kind is being heated, it must be stirred as soon as bubbles appear around the edges and again each time bubbling recurs. Always stir before serving to make sure that the temperature is even throughout.

Soup can be frozen in the bowl provided you can spare that item of crockery. The thawing and reheating method is exactly the same as reheating alone but it will obviously take a little longer. I would definitely recommend covering with vented cling film which helps the frozen area in the middle to defrost. Soup which has been frozen in a box will be a solid square shape so make sure that this will fit into the bowl and not prop up against one side – in this eventuality, during thawing the overlapping section will drip on to the oven shelf or turntable.

Cooking times for packet soups are determined by their type. Fragments of dehydrated vegetables or meat take longer to reconstitute than the powdered type. More time will therefore be needed for the former and softening can either be achieved by allowing a 10-minute soaking period in the added water or by increasing the cooking time. Remember that if you want just a single portion from a packet the ingredients must be accurately measured.

Speedy soups can be produced using cans as a basis. Simply add a little extra water, a spoonful or two or frozen or cooked vegetables, raw pasta shapes or chopped cooked meat or chicken and allow an extra 2 or 3 minutes reheating time. Raw ingredients such as rice or pearl barley will take much longer to cook and absorb even more liquid, but they do result in a more substantial meal. All these additions certainly relieve the monotony and taste and texture of most canned soups.

Cook soups in a fairly large bowl to allow for boiling up and choose ingredients that are less likely to form a scum. Bone broths and some dried peas and beans are inclined to do this. Vegetables should be chopped as small as possible with only enough liquid to cover them.

The quick and easy way to make smooth soups is to prepare a thin white sauce first and then add puréed cooked vegetables such as spinach, courgettes, carrots, beetroot, mushrooms or puréed raw cucumber. Cook them for 5 minutes.

Chicken stock makes an excellent base for quick soups. Make your stock from chicken skin and bones, a bay leaf, seasoning and a little piece of carrot and onion if possible. Put these ingredients into a 1.95 litre (3½ pint) bowl, add water to cover, then three-quarters cover the bowl with cling film and cook on Full Power for 20–30

minutes. Strain the liquid into another bowl and discard
the bones, skin and flavourings. Cool the stock as rapidly
as possible, then chill until a layer of fat forms on the
top. Remove this with a slotted spoon.

Chicken stock can be made at any convenient time, in
any quantity and will keep well in the freezer. If you
have no freezer space, keep it in a cool place but it must
be well and truly boiled up each day to prevent it from
becoming rancid.

Save the liquid from boiled vegetables to use up as
stock in soups and to improve their flavour. Add tomato
purée and puréed cooked vegetables and finally thicken
with a 'beurre manié' (see below). Put the stock and any
other ingredients in a large bowl and cook, three-quarters
covered with cling film, on Full Power until bubbling
around the edges. Remove the cling film, stir and continue
cooking until the bubbles appear once more. Meanwhile,
make the beurre manié by blending a teaspoon of soft
margarine or softened butter with a teaspoon of flour to
form a paste. Whisk this into the boiling soup – the soup
will then be creamier and thicker. To thicken the soup
even further add another teaspoon of beurre manié.

Soups are the most adaptable of all microwave recipes
so that the occasional missing ingredient won't matter.
You can achieve quite a variety simply by adding different
herbs, although one of the problems for the single person
is that after prolonged storage bottles of dried herbs tend
to discolour and lose their aroma. You can of course dry
your own herbs which will keep for some time. They
must be dried a handful at a time (without their stalks)
and require frequent stirring during the drying process.

Finally, I would like to remind you that soups do not
have to be reserved for cold weather. Many are just as
good eaten cold and the sauce-based kind lend themselves
admirably to summer eating.

THE RECIPES

QUICK COOKING

Cream of Spinach
Cream of Tomato
Chicken Velouté

MODERATELY QUICK COOKING

Celery Soup
Cream of Chicken Soup with
  Carrot and Celery
Kidney Soup

Minestrone
Smoky Cabbage Soup
Vichyssoise

SLOWER COOKING

French Onion Soup
Fresh Vegetable Soup

Fropack Vegetable Soup
Lentil Soup

CREAM OF SPINACH SOUP

To obtain a really creamy well-blended soup, I make use
of the liquidizer or blender. The food processor will do a
fairly good job so if you don't object to the texture of a
few separate spinach particles, there is no need to bother
with either a liquidizer or a blender.

The recipe makes two reasonable-sized servings and
the soup can be served cold, or reheated for about 3
minutes in a suitable soup bowl. Stir once during and
again at the end of reheating to make sure the heat is
evenly distributed.

  1 level tablespoon butter or soft margarine
  2 level tablespoons flour

150 ml (¼ pint) water
⅛ or tiny piece chicken stock cube
1 small piece onion, peeled and crushed
150 g (5 oz) freshly cooked, frozen or canned spinach
Salt
Freshly ground black pepper
Grated nutmeg
150 ml (¼ pint) milk

1.95 litre (3½ pint) bowl

Put the butter or margarine in a 1.95 litre (3½ pint) bowl
and without covering cook on Full Power for 30 seconds
or until melted. Stir in the flour, then add the water,
stock cube and onion and cook uncovered on Full Power
for 2 minutes or until beginning to bubble.

Whisk vigorously, then add the spinach, and the salt,
pepper and nutmeg to taste. Cook uncovered on Full
Power for a further 3 minutes (beating every minute) or
until boiling. Stir in the milk, then without covering cook
on Full Power for 2½ minutes or until just bubbling,
then stir and cook for a further minute.

Purée in the liquidizer if a creamy soup is desired.

CREAM OF TOMATO SOUP

A home-made soup somewhat reminiscent of the canned
variety but with fewer additives.

1 small piece onion, peeled
200 ml (7 fl oz) canned tomato juice
7 tablespoons water
Dash Worcestershire sauce
1 level teaspoon soft margarine
1 level teaspoon plain flour
Salt

Freshly ground black pepper
1 tablespoon double cream

1 litre (1¾ pint) bowl

Put the onion into a 1 litre (1¾ pint) bowl, cover with a soup bowl and cook on Full Power for 2 minutes or until the onion is soft.

Add the tomato juice, water and Worcestershire sauce and, without covering, cook on Full Power for 3 minutes or until the soup boils. Remove and discard the onion.

In a small bowl blend the margarine and the flour, then whisk into the boiling soup using a fork. Cook, uncovered, on Full Power for 2 minutes or until the soup returns to the boil.

Season to taste with salt and pepper, stir in the cream and serve hot.

CHICKEN VELOUTÉ

This is a delicious cream soup, although made with simple ingredients.

1 level tablespoon unsalted butter
1 level tablespoon plain flour
300 ml (½ pint) boiling water
½ chicken stock cube
2 level tablespoons double cream
White pepper
1 level teaspoon chopped chives, dried or fresh

1 litre (1¾ pint) bowl

Put the butter into a 1 litre (1¾ pint) bowl and cook, uncovered, on Full Power for 30 seconds or until melted. Stir in the flour and cook for 20–30 seconds or until the mixture puffs up.

Using a hand whisk stir in the water, then add the stock cube. Without covering, cook on Full Power for 1 minute then whisk thoroughly and cook for a further minute or until the soup is boiling. Whisk thoroughly and leave for 30 seconds, then whisk in the cream.

Season to taste with pepper. Stir in the chives and serve hot.

CELERY SOUP

The 12 minutes' cooking time should be sufficient for the vegetables but celery tends to remain slightly crunchy. Our testers liked the texture and therefore I am not recommending a longer cooking time.

2–3 celery stalks, topped, tailed and strings removed
1 small onion, peeled
1 small potato, peeled and diced
150 ml (¼ pint) boiling water
1 level teaspoon butter
150 ml (¼ pint) milk
Salt
Freshly ground black pepper

1.95 litre (3½ pint) bowl

Slice the celery and onion finely and put into a 1.95 litre (3½ pint) bowl with the diced potatoes, then add the water and butter.

Cover the bowl with vented cling film and cook on Full Power for 11–12 minutes or until the vegetables are tender.

Purée the soup in the liquidizer, then return the mixture to the bowl and stir in the milk.

Without covering, cook on Full Power for 4 minutes or until the soup is boiling. Season with salt and pepper and stir once before serving.

CREAM OF CHICKEN SOUP WITH CARROT AND CELERY

The soup is quickly cooked because of the way that the vegetables are prepared. In this recipe 'finely sliced' really means sliced wafer thin. (Celery is particularly slow to cook.) The carrots should be coarsely grated but then it is unlikely that you would be willing to slice two of the vegetables and then have to grate the third one. As a substitute for coarse grating, you can top, tail and scrape the carrots, then shred them finely using a potato peeler. The first few peelings may be fairly wide but after this you will find that you can obtain thin julienne strips by peeling along the squared-off or uneven edges. Peel the strips from the whole length of the carrot.

This recipe makes a generous 300ml (½ pint) and is a very substantial soup which would be acceptable as a light meal served with chunks of wholemeal French bread and butter.

1 chicken breast, skinned and finely diced
1 small piece onion, peeled and finely sliced
1 small carrot, coarsely grated
1 stick celery, finely sliced
300 ml (½ pint) water
4 tablespoons evaporated milk
2 level teaspoons cornflour
Salt
Freshly ground black pepper

1.95 litre (3½ pint) bowl

Mix the chicken, vegetables and 150ml (¼ pint) water in a 1.95 litre (3½ pint) bowl and cook, without covering, on Full Power for 4–5 minutes until the chicken is tender.

Stir in the evaporated milk. Blend the cornflour with a

little of the remaining water, then add to the vegetables with the rest of the water.

Season well with salt and pepper. Cook, uncovered, on Full Power for 8–10 minutes, stirring once or twice during cooking.

KIDNEY SOUP

This makes a generous 375 ml (12 fl oz) so that with the addition of a little extra stock, you could have enough for two servings. The soup freezes well and if you are not desperately short of crockery, you could freeze part of it in a soup bowl (securely covered in cling film) for a few days.

100 g (4 oz) of kidney
1 small onion, peeled and finely chopped
1 level tablespoon flour
Salt
Freshly ground black pepper
¼ level teaspoon dried thyme or other herbs
300 ml (½ pint) hot water
½ beef stock cube, crumbled
½ level tablespoon mushroom ketchup
1 teaspoon sherry

1.95 litre (3½ pint) bowl

Wash the kidney in cold salted water, rinse, then dry and chop finely. Put into a 1.95 litre (3½ pint) bowl and stir in the other ingredients in the order given. (It is better to add the dry ingredients before any liquid because this prevents lumpiness.)

Three-quarters cover the bowl with cling film and cook on Full Power for 15 minutes, stirring after about 3 minutes and then once or twice during the remaining cooking time. The mixture appears to separate slightly during cooking but comes together when beaten. (It is important to use a large bowl even though you are only cooking a small quantity because the soup tends to boil up.)

When the soup is cooked add a little extra boiling water or stock if you find that the consistency too thick for your liking.

MINESTRONE

This recipe makes about 450 ml (¾ pint) and is a very substantial meal indeed. In fact if the soup is left standing for any length of time it becomes much thicker. You can remedy this by adding extra boiling water or stock. Left-over soup will freeze or can be kept in the refrigerator for two or three days. Three-quarters cover the soup when reheating, which can be done on Full Power, and stir as soon as you see bubbles appearing around the sides. After thawing the soup will take about 3 minutes to reach eating temperature.

1 rasher back bacon, derinded and chopped
1 small onion, peeled and finely chopped
2 heaped tablespoons mixed diced vegetables (fresh, frozen or canned)
1 heaped tablespoon baked beans in tomato sauce
25 g (1 oz) quick-cooking macaroni
About 450 ml (¾ pint) hot water ⎫ or 450 ml (¾ pint)
¼ chicken stock cube, crumbled ⎭ chicken stock
Small piece cabbage, shredded (optional)
Salt
Freshly ground black pepper
1 level tablespoon grated cheese

1.25 litre (2¼ pint) casserole

Put the bacon and onion into a 1.25 litre (2¼ pint) casserole and cook, without covering, on Full Power for 2–3 minutes, stirring once during cooking.

Add the vegetables, baked beans, macaroni, stock and cabbage (if using), cover with the lid and cook on Full Power for 5 minutes or until you see the mixture boiling. Stir, then replace the lid (but leave a gap to prevent boiling over) and cook on Full Power for 10–12 minutes or until the soup is cooked and all the ingredients are tender.

Season with salt and pepper, but be careful not to overdo the salt particularly if the bacon is salty and if you have used a stock cube.

Stir in the cheese and serve with croûtons (page 214).

SMOKY CABBAGE SOUP

Unlikely combination of ingredients but one which produces an unusual and substantial soup. The recipe calls for cooked cabbage but it is equally acceptable to use freshly shredded raw cabbage (you will need about 100 g (4 oz)).

2 heaped tablespoons cooked cabbage
¼ green pepper, seeded and finely chopped
1 tomato, sliced
Small piece onion, peeled and finely chopped
2 slices German sausage, skinned and chopped
300 ml (½ pint) water
¼ level teaspoon caraway seeds (optional)
Freshly ground black pepper
Salt

1 litre (1¾ pint) bowl

Mix all the ingredients together in a 1 litre (1¾ pint)

bowl. Three-quarters cover with cling film and cook on Full Power for 15 minutes or until the cabbage is tender.

Purée the mixture in the liquidizer if you prefer a smoother soup, then season to taste with salt and pepper.

If the soup has been puréed, return it to the bowl and reheat, uncovered, for 2–3 minutes, stirring before serving.

VICHYSSOISE

A traditional soup made of leek and potato normally served cold but equally pleasant when served hot. This makes a generous 300 ml (½ pint); if the soup seems to be too thick, you can always add a little boiling water.

1 small onion, peeled and finely chopped
1 × 75 g (3 oz) potato, peeled and finely diced
1 × 75–100 g (3–4 oz) leek, trimmed and shredded, not sliced
300 ml (½ pint) water
¼ chicken stock cube
¼ teaspoon lemon juice
Salt and pepper
1 tablespoon double cream

1 litre (1¾ pint) bowl

Combine the onion, potato and leek in a 1 litre (1¾ pint) bowl. Cover with vented cling film and cook on Full Power for 5 minutes, shaking the bowl vigorously once during cooking (you will need oven gloves for this).

Remove the cling film, stir in the water, stock cube and lemon juice. Three-quarters cover with cling film, leaving a gap for stirring, and cook on Full Power for 10 minutes, stirring occasionally.

Purée the soup in the liquidizer, adding an extra 2

tablespoons of water. Return the soup to the bowl and, without covering, reheat for 3–4 minutes, then stir thoroughly to equalize the heat throughout.

Season to taste and stir in the cream just before serving.

FRENCH ONION SOUP

1 large or 2 medium onions, peeled and finely sliced
1 small clove garlic, peeled and finely crushed
2 teaspoons vegetable oil
2 level teaspoons flour
300 ml (½ pint) hot beef stock, or hot water and ¼
    beef stock cube, crumbled
4 tablespoons medium red wine
Dash Worcestershire sauce
Freshly ground black pepper
1 thick slice French bread, buttered on both sides
1 level tablespoon grated Parmesan cheese
2–3 level teaspoons grated Cheddar cheese
Salt

1.95 litre (3½ pint) bowl

Stir the onion, garlic and oil together in a 1.95 litre (3½ pint) bowl and, without covering, cook on Full Power for 7–8 minutes. Stir two or three times during cooking to mix the browner with the paler parts of the onion. The onion should be soft and beginning to brown.

Stir in the flour and cook on Full Power for 2–3 minutes until it becomes a light beige colour.

Add the stock, wine, Worcestershire sauce, a generous shake of black pepper and the Parmesan cheese. Three-quarters cover with cling film and cook on Full Power for 10 minutes, stirring occasionally. The soup should now have thickened and the onion become tender.

Remove the bowl from the microwave but leave the cling film in position.

Place the buttered bread on a plate or on the microwave shelf and, without covering, cook on Full Power for 1 minute. Sprinkle the top with the Cheddar cheese and continue cooking for 15–20 seconds until the cheese is melted.

Put the bread in the soup plate, season the soup with salt to taste and pour over the bread.

FRESH VEGETABLE SOUP

Most greengrocers will sell you a single vegetable but supermarkets often have ready packed mixed fresh root vegetables.

225 g (½ lb) prepared, peeled vegetables, e.g. 1
   medium onion, 1 medium carrot and 1 medium
   potato
1 tablespoon vegetable oil
300 ml (½ pint) hot water
Dash Worcestershire sauce
¼ level teaspoon bay leaf powder
Salt
Freshly ground black pepper

1.95 litre (3½ pint) bowl

Peel and finely chop the onion and mix with the oil in a 1.95 litre (3½ pint) bowl and, without covering, cook on Full Power for 3 minutes.

Meanwhile scrape and finely slice the carrot, peel and dice the potato. Stir these into the onion mixture, then mix in the water, Worcestershire sauce and seasonings.

Three-quarters cover the bowl with cling film and cook

on Full Power for 10–15 minutes or until the vegetables are tender.

Purée the soup in the blender or liquidizer or press through a sieve. Reheat, uncovered, for 3 minutes on Full Power. Stir before serving.

FROPACK VEGETABLE SOUP

Packs of mixed frozen vegetables (weighing 225–300 g (8–10 oz)) are readily available and they come in a variety of mixtures. Some are diced and some are in larger pieces, whilst stir-fry vegetables are finely sliced. A whole pack is sufficient for 2 generous portions but it is just as easy, and quicker, to make a single serving and store the other half of the vegetables in the freezer compartment of the refrigerator. However, I have given recipes for both quantities.

If preferred, liquidize the soup after cooking and then, without covering, reheat for 1–2 minutes on Full Power.

Single serving:
½ × 225 g (8 oz) pack mixed frozen or stir-fry
    vegetables
1 bay leaf
¼ teaspoon Bovril or Marmite
½ teaspoon tomato purée
Salt
Pepper
2 level teaspoons cornflour
5 tablespoons cold milk

1 litre (1¾ pint) bowl

Mix together the vegetables and about 210 ml (7½ fl oz) hot water in a 1 litre (1¾ pint) bowl. Add the bay leaf, Bovril or Marmite, tomato purée and season with salt and pepper. Cover with vented cling film and cook on Full Power for 8 minutes or until the vegetables are soft.

Blend the cornflour with the milk, pour the mixture into the soup and, without covering, cook for about 2 minutes or until bubbling occurs around the edges. Stir, then continue cooking for a further 3 minutes until bubbles reappear and the soup thickens.

Remove the bay leaf and adjust the seasoning, stirring before pouring into the serving bowl.

Double serving:
1 × 225–300 g (8–10 oz) pack mixed diced frozen or
　　stir-fry vegetables
1 bay leaf
½ teaspoon Bovril or Marmite
1 teaspoon tomato purée
Salt
Pepper
1 level tablespoon cornflour
150 ml (¼ pint) cold milk

Empty the vegetables into a 1.95 litre (3½ pint) bowl and add 450 ml (¾ pint) hot water, the bay leaf, Bovril or Marmite and tomato purée. Season with salt and pepper.

Cover with vented cling film and cook on Full Power for 12 minutes or until the vegetables are soft.

Blend the cornflour with 2 tablespoons of the milk, stir into the soup mixture, then mix in the remaining milk.

Cook, without covering, on Full Power for about 3 minutes or until bubbles appear around the edges. Stir, then continue cooking until bubbles reappear and the soup thickens.

Remove the bay leaf, adjust the seasoning and ladle into the serving bowl. Leave the remaining soup to cool, then refrigerate and reheat next day.

LENTIL SOUP

Fortunately lentils are one of the few pulses that don't
have to be pre-soaked, so the cooking is speeded up
considerably. Substitute green lentils or split peas to ring
the changes.

> 5 level tablespoons red lentils, rinsed and drained
> 750 ml (1¼ pint) hot beef stock, or boiling water plus
>   ¼ beef stock cube, crumbled
> 1 bacon rasher, derinded and chopped
> Small piece onion, peeled and finely chopped
> ¼ level teaspoon celery seed
> Knob of butter
> Salt
> Freshly ground black pepper
>
> 1.95 litre (3½ pint) bowl

Put the rinsed lentils into a 1.95 litre (3½ pint) bowl, add
the remaining ingredients and stir thoroughly.

Three-quarters cover the bowl with cling film and cook
on Full Power for 30–35 minutes, stirring occasionally
during cooking.

Purée the soup in the liquidizer. Reheat, without covering, for 1 minute or until soup bubbles around the edges.
Stir then reheat for a further 30–45 seconds. Stir again
before serving.

Main Courses

Main courses are more difficult to construct than starters as, apart from cold meats and salad, the ingredients need cooking. In the microwave this is very simple to accomplish and you can choose from a wide range of basics including chops, steaks, burgers, chicken quarters and fish fillets, along with a couple of fresh vegetables to be quickly and nutritiously cooked to accompany them.

In the recipes in this chapter you will find some quick-cooking, some medium-quick-cooking and some slow-cooking dishes; a choice of fish, poultry, meat and some dishes suitable for the vegetarian. Many of these are composite dishes with vegetables cooked in with the main ingredients, so that all you need for accompaniment is a hunk of bread.

Portion sizes are difficult to decide on as some people have larger appetites than others. A starter before and a dessert afterwards will make the meal seem even more filling.

All the main-course recipes are reasonably easy to prepare but if you want to add extra vegetables, pre-cook them (to the tender not soft stage, by slightly reducing the given cooking time) and then reheat them on the dish with the main course. When you are preparing a plain meal like sausages, mashed potato and cabbage, you can of course cook extra sausages if you wish.

The main problems with microwave cooking arise from menu planning – not so much what you eat, but how to organize the meal so that it all arrives hot at the same time. It is quite impossible to cook everything all at once unless it is a meal-in-one-dish.

To plan a meal as a whole, there are lots of cold starters which do not necessarily require any cooking and which can be prepared in advance or while the main course is cooking. You could choose from: melon; grapefruit; avocado; prawn cocktail; cold salamis and meats; bought-in or home-made pâtés and salads.

The hot main meal could then be followed by a similarly easy cold dessert (see the Desserts chapter for recipes which can be prepared in advance in the microwave). Fresh fruit or cheese and biscuits never go amiss, of course.

Chops and steaks: To cook mouthwatering lamb chops and beef steaks in the microwave you will need to use either a browning dish or part cook them in an ordinary dish and finish in the frying pan or under the grill.

Cooking in the Browning Dish:
Preheat the empty unlidded browning dish to the maximum recommended by the manufacturer. Quickly add a marble-sized knob of butter or a tablespoon of vegetable oil. Press the chop or steak on to the hot surface, cook for 30 seconds, then turn the meat over, pushing it around the dish with tongs or a fork so that maximum use is made of the entire hot surface. Continue cooking according to the chart below.

Chops and steaks need a short cooking period followed by a short standing time.

Lamb chops	150 g (5 oz)	1 minute on either side (allow 1½ minutes each side if cooking 2 chops)

Thick lamb chops	175 g (6 oz)	1¼ minutes on either side (allow 2 minutes each side if cooking 2 chops)
Pork Chops	225 g (8 oz)	1½ minutes on first side, 3–4 minutes on second side
Steaks	2½ cm (1 in) thick	*Rare* 1 minute on either side *Medium* 1¼ minutes on either side *Well done* 2 minutes on either side

Chops can be cooked in an ordinary dish, in which case you will either have to cook them in a sauce or colour them brown with Bisto, tomato ketchup, HP sauce, gravy browning or microwave seasoning.

Trim away any surplus fat and cook on Defrost (30 per cent). Put the seasoned or sauced chop(s) in the dish and cover with greaseproof or kitchen paper. Allow a cooking time of 6–8 minutes per chop on Defrost (30 per cent).

Casseroles: Cheap coarse cuts of meat do not lend themselves to microwave cookery as microwaves cannot tenderize. The resultant textures are more similar to grilled or fried meat.

To prepare beef or lamb for casseroles, cut the meat into small even-sized dice; alternatively marinate for several hours prior to cooking with tenderizing powder (an enzyme from the pawpaw) and leave for 30 minutes. Cook on the Defrost (30 per cent) setting and extend the cooking time.

Casseroles cooked by microwave *do* improve if rapidly cooled and set aside for several hours before reheating. (Plunge the base of the casserole into a bowl of cold water and stir the food as it cools. Replace the cold water as its temperature increases.) Reheat, covered, on Full Power and stir occasionally.

Chicken casseroles can be cooked on Full Power. Minced or chopped meat can be cooked rapidly because mincing or chopping is a natural method of tenderizing. Mince takes about 5 minutes per 450 g (1 lb) on Full Power. (Raw mince does not keep very well so buy only the quantity you need at any one time.)

Roasts: Large joints will brown because they are cooked for a prolonged period and the fat, which gets progressively hot, breaks through the surface of the meat.

Big lumps of meat don't cook evenly all the way through and can become exceedingly dry outside. A lone diner is better off because he will require only a small joint, probably not more than 900 g (2 lb). Although this size of joint won't brown the texture will be superior.

To cook in the microwave oven, preheat the browning dish as per the manufacturer's instructions then rapidly brown the joint on all sides, turning it with tongs and pushing it against the hot surface of the dish. Having done this, leave the joint in the dish and cook on Full Power for 7–8 minutes per 450 g (1 lb).

Alternatively, put the joint on a rack in a shallow dish, cover with a split roasting bag and cook on Full Power for a slightly longer period per 450 g (1 lb), then brown under the grill.

If your oven is equipped with a probe, insert this into the centre of the joint after putting it in the microwave and set the temperature to 55°C (130°F). (A meat thermometer will register the internal temperature if inserted during or after cooking but do not allow an ordinary meat thermometer to remain in the meat throughout the cooking period as the mercury would burst out and, being metal, would damage the oven as well as ruining the thermometer.) After the minimum cooking time tent the joint with vented foil and leave for about 10 minutes. During this time the heat will equalize throughout.

The average cooking time on Full Power required for a 450 g (1 lb) joint of beef is

Rare	5 minutes	Internal temperature after standing 60°C (140°F)
Medium	7 minutes	Internal temperature after standing 70°C (160°F)
Well done	8 minutes	Internal temperature after standing 75°C (170°F)
For other types of meat the times are		
Lamb	8–10 minutes	Internal temperature after standing 80°C (175°F)
Veal	8½–9 minutes	Internal temperature after standing 75°C (170°F)
Pork	9–10 minutes	Internal temperature after standing 80°C (175°F)

Ideally joints should be turned over half-way through cooking. If the bone has been left in joints, the meat will cook more quickly as the bone will conduct heat. If the joint is unevenly shaped, e.g. a leg of lamb, to avoid burning, shield the bone end with foil overwrapped with cling film.

You will soon be able to judge the appropriate cooking times applicable to your particular microwave oven and then there will be no need to bother with temperature tests.

Liver and Kidneys: Slice, remove the sinews and core. Cook on a plate or in a dish covered with vented cling film or non-stick paper on Full Power. Stir or reposition during cooking. Allow about 6–7 minutes per 450g (1 lb).

Poultry: All poultry, provided it is of good quality, whether whole or jointed, whether casseroled or roasted is tender and succulent when cooked in the microwave oven. Happily the single person can buy chicken prepared in several ways so that thighs, drumsticks, breasts (with skins or skinless), chicken quarters and chicken halves are all available. Duck quarters, whole poussins and turkey fillets are on sale in the larger supermarkets all year round. The smallest whole chicken weighs about 1 kg (2¼ lb) and will do for at least two meals, which is good value at reasonable cost.

Roast chicken: To thaw a frozen bird remove the metal tag, slit the bag underneath and put the whole pack in a shallow dish. Defrost on 20 per cent power (or no. 2 if your oven has variable control) or on Defrost (30 per cent) if this is the lowest setting available. Allow about 9 minutes per 450 g (1 lb) on 20 per cent power and 6 minutes 450 g (1 lb) on Defrost (30 per cent). As soon as the chicken has thawed sufficiently, pull out the giblets and plunge the bird into a bowl of cold water until no ice can be felt inside the cavity.

Drain the chicken and put on an upturned undecorated saucer in a suitable dish (or on a microwave rack in the dish). Rub the skin with butter and sprinkle with microwave seasoning or paprika if you wish to have a brownish finish. Cover with a split roasting bag or lid and cook on Full Power for 6 minutes. Reduce the setting to Defrost (30 per cent) and cook for a further 15–20 minutes or until the bone in the leg can be twisted and pulled out easily. Preferably leave to stand, covered, for 10 minutes before jointing or slicing.

The finished temperature should read 90°C (190°F). Another reliable test is to insert a sharp knife into the chicken between the thigh and the body – the juices should run clear when sufficiently cooked. After roasting brown the chicken under the grill.

Use the carcass and skin to make chicken stock.

Chicken portions: These, whether boned or not, will pop during cooking as the sinews, being little enclosed pockets, expand. This is not noticeable when cooking a whole chicken as these are deep inside the flesh. When cooking chicken portions use non-stick paper, a lid or vented cling film, depending on whether you want soft and moist or drier results. Unless the poultry is oiled or buttered I would not recommend greaseproof paper as it is inclined to stick.

Cook the poultry pieces on Full Power (unless the recipe states otherwise) and turn them over half-way through cooking. Allow 2–2½ minutes for one boneless breast and 3–4 minutes for a joint. Leg quarters usually take longer than breast quarters.

Poultry skin does not become crisp and since the fatty part is located just under the skin, it is as well to remove it before cooking (unless you are roasting poultry). Cooking time is then reduced because the microwaves can concentrate on the flesh and not on the melted fat.

Use the skin and bones before or after roasting to make chicken stock. When well flavoured this turns into an excellent chicken soup, providing an extra meal but without extra expense.

Fish: This is always a good main meal choice and is excellent when cooked in the microwave oven. It isn't greasy, it cooks quickly, and the smell will not permeate the room as in conventional cooking. Fish is nutritious and easy to buy in suitable 'single' portions.

Fresh fish is best, of course, and among your choices are fillets, cutlets, small whole fish (including herrings, trout, plaice and sole). The amount of trouble you go to depends on you, but all can be cooked on the dinner plate without further adornment. Season with salt and pepper and add a sprinkling of lemon juice or a dab of butter, then cover with non-stick paper or vented cling film and allow 3½–4 minutes to 450 g (1 lb). If the heads have been removed the timing will be even shorter.

I usually use cling film to cover fillets and cutlets, and non-stick paper to cover whole fish. Herrings need not be turned over, but trout will cook more evenly if you do this. For special occasions you may like to wrap a small piece of smooth foil over the tail end of a whole fish to prevent overcooking. The tail end of a fillet can be folded under to even out the thickness.

'Doneness' is easy to recognize in fillets or cutlets because the flesh turns opaque and breaks apart when flaked with a fork. Whole fish must be tested by inserting a sharp knife into the thickest part which, when cooked, should offer no resistance. A warning sign of overcooking is when you hear more than a little popping – you will notice shrinkage, drying up and tiny specks of congealed white lumps on the surface. Since fish does cook so rapidly, on your first attempt you should stay nearby so that you can interrupt the cooking cycle to test how well the fish is cooking.

Use up the bones, head and any bits of skin to make fish stock – another microwave winner.

Apart from fish fingers, fish steaks and breaded portions, always thaw frozen fish before cooking so that you won't end up with a raw section in the middle. Thaw on Defrost (30 per cent) for all except large whole flat fish such as plaice and sole, allowing 3 minutes per 450 g (1 lb). When the fish is still board-like, but slightly 'bendy', finish the thawing in cold water. Large fish should be thawed on the lowest setting (10 per cent or no. 1), allowing 5–6 minutes to each 450 g (1 lb). If the lowest setting on your microwave oven is Defrost (30 per cent), then after 2½–3 minutes, give a 10-minute rest before completing the thawing process.

All fish, whether starting from frozen, after thawing, or fresh, can be cooked entirely on Defrost (30 per cent). Allow about 13–14 minutes per 450 g (1 lb) from frozen and 10 minutes per 450 g (1 lb) when fresh or thawed.

Shellfish: The Japanese, who are great shellfish experts, are also microwave enthusiasts. The two go together well.

Lobster has usually been cooked by the fishmonger, although it can be cooked in the microwave. A whole small lobster feeds one person, so when you want to treat yourself try Lobster Thermidor (see page 75). If you can't get fresh lobster, frozen lobster meat is excellent.

Crabmeat is obtainable in a frozen block but this is probably too big for one serving. You are more likely to purchase a whole crab which will be ready cooked, unless of course you are a fisherman yourself.

Among other pre-cooked (either frozen or freshly cooked) shellfish are prawns. If you wish to use these in cooked dishes, add them towards the end of cooking time to ensure that they won't be overcooked. They take very little cooking and overcooking makes them tough.

To thaw frozen raw scampi, scallops and prawns, put them in a circle in a dish and cover with two or three thicknesses of kitchen paper. A considerable amount of water results from thawing and the kitchen paper will soak it up. Remove each piece of shellfish as soon as it is defrosted.

Preferably cook raw small shelled or soft-shelled seafoods such as prawns, scampi, scallops and lobster tails on Defrost (30 per cent), stirring or turning over frequently. A 225 g (8 oz) lobster tail will take about 3 minutes, 100 g (4 oz) prawns about 2½ minutes and two shelled scallops about 2 minutes. The times are very short and if you try and cook a small number on Full Power there is a very real risk of overcooking.

Oysters are so expensive that I would hesitate to make any hard and fast rules but on the other hand fresh mussels can be cooked very simply – just make sure that you remove each mussel from the cooking container as soon as it has opened. Twelve mussels cooked in hot liquid on Full Power are ready to serve in about 2 minutes.

Eggs and Cheese: Eggs and cheese are commonly used in vegetable and vegetarian main meals.

If scrambled eggs are cooked with additional ingredients, allow a little more cooking time.

Raw shelled eggs can be cooked in the hollowed-out centre of cooked spinach or ratatouille. Frozen or canned vegetables lend themselves to speedy cooking in this way. It is important to position the eggs correctly if you want to prevent them from bursting. If they are broken into the centre of the dish and surrounded by the cooked vegetables, savoury cooked rice or cooked pasta and perhaps topped with a spoonful of sauce, the intensity of the microwave action on the eggs will be reduced, enabling them to be cooked, covered, on Full Power. Otherwise they must be cooked on the defrost setting or be pricked prior to cooking. Left-over ingredients can be reheated in this way, with the addition of the egg to provide a good sustaining meal.

Shelled hard-boiled eggs are delicious served cold with salad, or halved and coated in a Hollandaise sauce which latter can be cooked by microwave.

Cheese melts quickly in the microwave and so cheese puddings and fondues are suitable for cooking this way.

When cooking cheese on its own use the Defrost (30 per cent) setting.

Vegetable main courses: Vegetable main courses should be nutritionally well balanced and are becoming popular because they provide the necessary dietary fibre (or 'roughage' as it used to be called). Other ingredients can be varied to provide a substantial meal for the vegetarian.

In the case of stuffed vegetables, bear in mind that since microwaves cook more around the edges, the sides may collapse if the recipe instructions are not strictly followed. This likelihood is more relevant to natural high-moisture-content vegetables such as tomatoes, marrow and aubergine. Peppers being drier are sturdier. When the empty cavity of the vegetable is being stuffed (the flesh being discarded) the cooking time will depend on the filling itself, but when the stuffing includes the pulp of the vegetable (as with potatoes) the vegetable should be cooked first. Mushrooms are stuffed by putting the filling on top of and not inside the vegetable, so that although their water content is high, they will *not* disintegrate.

When using cheese as a topping, add this after the dish is cooked and then brown under the grill. Dishes topped with grated cheese combined with fresh breadcrumbs can be cooked entirely by microwave. The topping will not brown but it will become crisp.

THE RECIPES

QUICK COOKING

---------------------- *FISH* ----------------------

Fresh Haddock Fillet with Leek Purée

Frozen Fish Fillets, Ready Crumbed

Haddock Granada

Kippers

Lobster Thermidor

Scampi in White Wine and Vodka

Trout

Trout en Papillote

Trout with Almonds

Whole or Filleted Smoked White Fish

---------------------- *MEAT* ----------------------

Beefburgers Rossini

Beef and Tomato Crumble

Egg and Corned Beef Hollow

Fillet Steak in Brown Sauce

Gammon, Pineapple and Peas

Ham and Egg Pie

Kidney, Mushrooms and Bacon in Red Wine Sauce

Lamb Chops in Ratatouille

Liver and Bacon Kebabs in Wine Sauce

Liver, Mushrooms and Tomato

Meat Balls in Canned Curry Sauce

Mince and Mushroom Crumble

Savoury Stuffed Peppers

Stuffed Green Pepper

Sweet and Sour Spare Ribs

Tangy Lemon Pork Chops

———————————— *POULTRY*————————————

Chicken à la King
Chicken Bordeaux
Chicken Breasts in Creamy
  Sauce

Turkey, Sweetcorn and
  Almond Fricassée

———————————— *VEGETABLE DISHES*————————————

Cheese Fondue
Cheese Pudding
Devilled Mushrooms
Field Mushrooms in Soy and
  Sherry Gravy
Mushrooms and Tomatoes in
  Sherry Sauce

Poached Soufflette
Savoury Rarebit
Spinach Omelette
Stuffed Jacket Potato

MODERATELY QUICK COOKING

———————————— *FISH*————————————

Coquilles St Jacques Savoyard
Prawn, Salmon and Tuna Quiche
Prawn and Tarragon Pilau

MEAT

Bacon and Onion Flan
Brown Beef and Onion
   Casserole
Carrot, Parsnip and Bacon
   Hotpot
Cider Rabbit
Lamb Ragôut

Moussaka
Pork, Kidney Bean and Apple
   Dinner
Sausage Risotto
Shepherd's Pie
Spring Lamb Chops

POULTRY

Chicken Kiev
Chicken Mussoori
Chicken and Olive Casserole

VEGETABLE DISHES

Cauliflower Cheese and Chives
Macaroni Cheese
Stuffed Aubergine

SLOWER COOKING

FISH

Not suitable for fish as fish cooks quickly

—————————*MEAT*—————————

Beef in Brown Ale
Caribbean Curry
Chilli Con Carne
Hungarian Goulash

Lamb Hotpot
Minced Beef Stroganoff
Steak and Kidney Pudding

—————————*POULTRY*—————————

Chicken in Green Pepper Sauce
Chicken and White Wine Casserole
Christmas Roast Duck

—————————*VEGETABLE DISHES*—————————

Kichkiri
Spinach and Cashew Nut Quiche

FRESH HADDOCK FILLET WITH LEEK PURÉE

Substitute any white fish fillet if you wish, although I think that haddock has the better flavour. The dish is reminiscent of nouvelle cuisine in style and appearance.

175–225 g (6–8 oz) fresh leeks
1 level teaspoon butter
4 tablespoons water
Salt
Freshly ground black pepper
150–175 g (5–6 oz) white fish fillet
Freshly chopped parsley to garnish

0.4 litre (¾ pint) pie dish

Wash, top, tail and finely slice the leeks. Place them in a 0.4 litre (¾ pint) pie dish with the butter and water and season generously with salt and pepper.

Skin the fish and put the skin, but not the fish, into the dish with the leeks (this is for added flavour). Cover with vented cling film and cook on Full Power for 5–7 minutes or until the leeks are cooked. Remove and discard the fish skin.

Without draining, purée the leeks in the food processor or blender, then pour the mixture back into the pie dish.

Place the fish on top of the leek purée and cover the dish with vented cling film. Cook on Full Power for approximately 2½ minutes or until the fish is white and flaky.

Carefully remove the cling film, sprinkle the chopped parsley over the fish and serve.

READY-CRUMBED FROZEN FISH FILLETS

The smallest packet that I have been able to obtain is 300 g (10.6 oz), which contains two fish fillets. Therefore the timings here are for a crumbed fillet weighing about 150 g (5 oz). If you have no freezer so that you have to cook both fillets, either cook one at a time (reheating the browning dish for 1 minute before cooking the second fillet) or, if the browning dish is big enough, cook them both together, increasing the cooking time by 2 minutes. Should the browning dish be an unsuitable size for a whole fillet you will need to cut the fillet in half. After cooking, if necessary the fish can be refrigerated or kept in a very cold place and subsequently reheated in the microwave oven on Full Power for about 30 seconds to 1 minute for a hot meal next day.

2 tablespoons vegetable oil
1 × 150 g (5 oz) ready-to-cook crumbed frozen white
  fish fillet

Browning dish

Put the oil in the cold browning dish and, without
covering, heat on Full Power for 3–4 minutes. Using a
fish slice immediately press the flesh side of the fish on to
the hot surface, then quickly turn on to the skin side.
Cook on Full Power for 3 minutes, then serve at once.

You can also cook ready-crumbed fish fillets in an ordinary microwave-proof dish but although the fillet will
look reasonably attractive, it will in no way be browned
or crisp.

HADDOCK GRANADA

Use any white fish fillet for this recipe, which can be
served with vegetables additional to those already in the
list of ingredients if you wish.

1 small clove garlic, peeled
15 g (½ oz) butter
2 tablespoons dry white wine
2 tablespoons water
1 sprig parsley
1 sprig rosemary
1 bay leaf
50 g (2 oz) frozen peas
50 g (2 oz) frozen cut beans
4 tablespoons double cream
175 g (6 oz) fresh haddock or cod fillet
Salt
White pepper
1 level teaspoon cornflour

1 tablespoon milk

Crushed puff pastry trimmings or micro-fried crumbs
    to garnish

1.25 litre (2¼ pint) casserole

Put the garlic, butter, wine, water, herbs, peas and beans
in a 1.25 litre (2¼ pint) casserole, cover with the lid and
cook on Full Power for 5 minutes. Remove the garlic and
herbs.

Stir in the cream, then add the fish seasoned with salt
and pepper. Baste the fish with the cream liquid, then
cook, without covering, on Full Power for 3 minutes or
until the fish is white and flaky.

Transfer the fish to a serving dish and surround with
the peas and beans which will need to be removed from
the dish with a slotted spoon.

Blend the cornflour with the milk, stir the mixture into
the juices left in the casserole and cook, without covering,
for 1 minute, stirring once during cooking until the sauce
thickens.

Adjust the seasoning, stir and pour the sauce over the
fish.

Sprinkle with the crushed pastry trimmings or micro-
fried crumbs and serve.

KIPPERS

1 large or 2 small kippers

Suitable plate

Put the large kipper on a suitable plate skin-side down,
cover with vented cling film and cook on Full Power for
2–3 minutes.

To cook two smaller kippers, overlap the tail ends and

slip a piece of greaseproof paper or cling film between the two fish so that they do not stick together. Cooking time will still be 2–3 minutes.

As the kippers cook, they arch their backs and the centre bones begin to draw away from the flesh. This is a sign of 'doneness'.

LOBSTER THERMIDOR

If you haven't a fishmonger within miles don't ignore frozen lobster which when thawed and cooked properly tastes the same, but remember to thaw the lobster meat thoroughly before cooking.

  1 small lobster or 100 g (4 oz) lobster meat
  25 g (1 oz) butter
  2 spring onions, topped, tailed and the white part finely
    chopped
  1 tablespoon dry white wine
  ¼ teaspoon freshly made mustard
  15 g (½ oz) flour
  150 ml (¼ pint) milk
  3 level tablespoons grated Gruyère cheese
  2 level teaspoons grated Parmesan cheese
  Yolk of 1 size 5 egg or ½ larger beaten egg

  1 litre (1¾ pint) bowl
  Lobster shells or individual flameproof dish

Cut up the lobster meat into small pieces and set aside.

Put 15 g (½ oz) of the butter into a 1 litre (1¾ pint) bowl and heat on Full Power for 30 seconds or until melted, then stir in the onions and cook for a further 30 seconds.

Add the wine and mustard, stir thoroughly, then mix

in the lobster meat and, without covering, heat on Full Power for 1 minute, stirring once half-way through cooking.

Transfer the mixture to another dish and set aside. Without covering, heat the remaining 12½ g (½ oz) butter for about 15 seconds. When melted, stir in the flour and cook for a further 15 seconds. Add the milk all at once and stir briefly with a wire whisk. Without covering, cook on Full Power for about 2 minutes (stirring every 30 seconds) or until the sauce is thick.

Add half the Gruyère and half the Parmesan cheese, beat in the egg yolk, then fold in the lobster mixture.

Spoon the mixture into the lobster shell or a flameproof dish, sprinkle with the remaining cheese and brown under the grill.

SCAMPI IN WHITE WINE AND VODKA

The sauce is intentionally thin but if you prefer a thicker sauce, you could increase the flour to one level tablespoon. A suitable substitution for the scampi are thawed cooked prawns and you can use brandy instead of vodka for flaming.

100 g (4 oz) deep-frozen scampi, thawed
Salt
Freshly ground black pepper
Shake garlic powder
½ level teaspoon flour
15 g (½ oz) butter or margarine
4 tablespoons medium white wine
1 tablespoon vodka

Shallow dish

Season the scampi with salt, pepper and the garlic powder, then toss them in the flour.

Put the butter or margarine in a shallow flameproof dish and heat, without covering, on Full Power for 30 seconds or until the butter is melted.

Stir in the scampi and pour the wine over the top. Cook, without covering, on Full Power for 2 minutes.

Stir and turn the scampi over and, still without covering, cook on Full Power for a further 1 minute.

Pour the vodka into a cup or ramekin and, without covering, heat on Full Power for 15 seconds. Pour the vodka over the scampi and ignite immediately.

If you wish to serve the scampi with rice, before flambéeing arrange the cooked rice in a border around the scampi and heat for 2 minutes, then warm the vodka, pour over the scampi and ignite.

TROUT

This is perhaps the microwave's favourite fish because it is not too thick and is already enclosed in its own natural wrapping – its skin.

Because of its shape and thickness it is essential to thaw frozen trout before cooking. To do this, slash through the immediate outer plastic wrapper once or twice, then put the packet, slit side down, on a plate to catch the drips. Thaw on the Defrost setting (30 per cent) for 2–3 minutes (for one trout), then remove the plastic wrapping and wash the fish in cold water before proceeding to cook.

Frozen large trout are less easy to obtain although you may of course purchase fresh fish and then freeze it yourself. In this case, remove all the wrappings before thawing as these are likely to be less suitable for microwave use than the commercial type. Put the fish in a dish or straight on to the turntable and heat on the Defrost setting (30 per cent) for 4 minutes. Turn the fish over and continue the process for a further 3–4 minutes. Wash the fish in cold water, removing any bits and pieces of the fish's innards that you might have missed before freezing.

Large trout are best cooked on the Defrost setting (30 per cent), allowing 10–12 minutes to the pound. Curve the fish round on the turntable or lay it flat in a dish on the microwave shelf, cover the head and tail with a smooth piece of foil, making sure that the foil is tucked inside the dish. If a dish is not being used, then overwrap the head and tail with cling film. Slash the skin once near the head and again near the tail and add a few dabs of butter. Cook entirely on the Defrost setting (30 per cent), removing the foil and cling film towards the end of the cooking time.

TROUT ON A PLATE

1 small trout weighing up to 300 g (10 oz)
Salt
Freshly ground black pepper
Squeeze lemon juice

Suitable plate

Put the fish on a suitable plate. Slash through the skin at the head and tail end and season with salt and pepper and sprinkle with the lemon juice.

Cover the fish with vented cling film and cook on Full Power for 2 minutes. Using a sharp knife pierce the thickest part of the fish through the cling film to test if the fish is cooked. Cook for a further minute if necessary.

TROUT EN PAPILLOTE

The advantage of this method of cooking is that you can remove the head and skin and fillet the fish all on the paper which can then be thrown away leaving you with no mess to clear up.

Larger trout will take slightly longer to cook.

1 × 8–10 oz (225–300 g) trout
Baking parchment (non-stick paper)

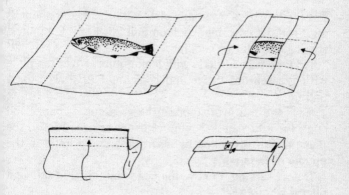

Rinse the thawed trout and wrap in a sheet of baking parchment.

Put the parcel in the microwave oven and cook on Full Power for 1½–2 minutes.

Open the wrapping and test the fish to see if it is cooked. If it is not quite cooked close the packet again and cook for a further minute.

Season with salt and pepper after cooking or serve with melted butter and finely chopped herbs.

TROUT WITH ALMONDS

Simple, easy and successful but frozen trout should be at least partially thawed before cooking.

25 g (1 oz) butter
1 level tablespoon flaked almonds
1 × 225g (8 oz) ready-to-cook trout
Squeeze lemon juice

Suitable plate

Put the butter on a suitable plate with the flaked almonds and, without covering, cook on Full Power for 2 minutes, stirring once during cooking.

Add the fish, sprinkle with lemon juice, cover the plate with greaseproof paper and cook on Full Power for 1 minute.

Turn the fish over, replace the greaseproof paper and cook for a further 1–2 minutes as necessary. Test to see that the fish is cooked by inserting a sharp knife in the middle of the flesh.

Before serving, remove the head and tail, and skin and fillet if you so wish.

WHOLE OR FILLETED SMOKED WHITE FISH

An average portion weighs 225 g (8 oz) but there is far more waste on whole smoked haddock than there is on fillets. Allow a cooking time of about 4 minutes per 450 g (1 lb) for fish which is at room temperature. Small compact shapes can be cooked from frozen, but any pieces that are much longer than they are broad should be thawed first. Do this on the plate or serving dish and then follow with the cooking period; 4 minutes on the Defrost setting (30 per cent) should be sufficient.

A frozen smoked fish portion weighing 225 g (8 oz) would therefore take 6 minutes, thawing/cooking time from freezer to table. If you do not want to go to the trouble of thawing on one setting and then cooking on another, you could thaw and cook entirely or consecutively on Defrost (30 per cent), when the total microwaving time would be about 10 minutes.

Sniff the fish before you cook it. This is not so much to see whether it is good or not, but rather to see whether it is salty. To cook salty fish place skin-side down in a dish and add two or three tablespoons of water, then cover the dish with vented cling film. Drain off the water when cooled. Otherwise put the fish directly on to the plate, cover with vented cling film and cook in the same way but there will be no need to drain.

To test whether the fish is cooked, press through the cling film covering when the fish should be flaky and almost opaque. Overcooked smoked fish becomes very dry, so don't over-estimate the time needed – you can always add an extra minute if the fish is insufficiently cooked when tested.

BEEFBURGER ROSSINI

Serve this as a lunch snack on its own or, if you want to make it even more substantial, cook two burgers, sandwich them together with pâté and increase the final cooking time by one minute. You can of course make your own burgers (see page 212).

1 slice crustless bread, buttered on both sides
1 × 75 g (3 oz) lean beefburger
25 g (1 oz) liver pâté
2 slices firm tomato

Browning dish

Preheat the empty unlidded browning dish to the maximum recommended by the manufacturer. Immediately press the buttered bread on to the hot surface and then turn it over and press similarly hard until the second side is also browned and crispened. Remove from the dish.

Reheat the browning dish for 30 seconds (it will not matter if it becomes discoloured). Press the burger flat on to the hot dish with a fish slice and immediately flip it over so that both sides of the burger are sealed and lightly browned. Remove from the dish.

Spread the pâté on one side of the bread, top with the burger and cover with the tomato slices.

Lift the topped toast carefully back into the browning dish (which will still be warm) and, without covering, cook on Full Power for 1 minute which should be just sufficient to cook the tomato. (The bread will absorb the juices from the burger and the pâté become very soft.)

BEEF AND TOMATO CRUMBLE

1 × 227 g (8 oz) can tomatoes
100 g (4 oz) lean raw minced beef
Salt
Freshly ground black pepper
Dash Worcestershire sauce
1 level teaspoon cornflour
50 g (2 oz) plain flour
25 g (1 oz) butter or margarine
1½ level teaspoons paprika
1 rounded tablespoon cornflakes

0.7 litre (1¼ pint) oval pie dish

Using a spoon or fork remove the tomatoes from the can without taking all the juice and mash them in a 0.7 litre

1¼ pint) oval pie dish with the beef, seasoning and a generous dash of Worcestershire sauce.

Blend the cornflour with the juice remaining in the can and pour over the beef mixture, forking it in lightly until absorbed.

Put the flour into a mixing bowl and add the butter or margarine cut into small pieces. Using your fingers rub the fat into the flour until the mixture resembles very fine crumbs. Stir in the paprika then crush the cornflakes and add these to the mixture.

Spoon the crumb mixture over the meat and pat down lightly with a palette knife or the back of a spoon. Place the dish in the microwave and cook on Full Power for about 7 minutes. The juices from the meat will rise up the sides of the dish to form a border.

EGG AND CORNED BEEF HOLLOW

You need about 100 g (4 oz) corned beef for this recipe but if you have to buy a tin rather than ready-sliced corned beef, the remainder will keep quite well in the refrigerator for a few days. You can then use it up as sandwich fillings, in corned beef hash or cook it with scrambled egg.

100 g (4 oz) corned beef
1 level teaspoon mild chilli sauce
1 egg
Corn chips (or potato crisps)

200 ml (7 fl oz) ramekin

Put the corned beef into a 200 ml (7 fl oz) ramekin and, without covering, cook on Full Power for 30 seconds.

Drain away any surplus fat, then press the meat into the sides and base of the dish to form a hollow.

Pour the chilli sauce into the hollow, spreading it with the bowl of a spoon. Break the egg into the centre of the hollow.

Cover the ramekin loosely with cling film (not vented), reduce the setting to Defrost (30 per cent) and cook for about 4 minutes or until the egg is cooked to your satisfaction. The egg yolk will continue cooking after the dish is removed from the oven, so do not overcook.

Sprinkle with crumbled corn chips or potato crisps just before serving.

FILLET STEAK IN BROWN SAUCE

The sauce makes about 300 ml (½ pint) and would probably do for two servings. It is equally good with lamb chops or chicken portions and it also freezes well.

25 g (1 oz) butter
1 small onion, peeled and finely chopped
3 level tablespoons flour
1 × 285 g (10 oz) can condensed beef consommé
¼ level teaspoon dry mustard powder
1 level tablespoon tomato purée
2 tablespoons double cream
Knob of butter
1 thick fillet steak

1 litre (1¾ pint) bowl
Small browning dish

Put the butter in a 1 litre (1¾ pint) bowl and, without covering, cook on Full Power for 30 seconds until melted.

Stir in the onion and cook, without covering, on Full Power for 2 minutes, then add the flour. (The mixture will look very lumpy.)

Stir in the consommé, mustard powder and tomato

purée and cook on Full Power, stirring frequently with a wooden spoon for 2 minutes or until the sauce thickens.

Stir in the cream and cook for another 30 seconds. Remove from the oven and cover to keep warm while preparing the steak.

Preheat an unlidded small browning dish for the maximum time recommended by the manufacturer. Quickly add a knob of butter, then press the steak on to the hot surface using a fish slice or tongs. Quickly turn the steak over, press once again against the hot surface and, without covering, cook on Full Power for 1 minute for 'rare'. If on cutting the steak it is found to be insufficiently cooked, reheat the browning dish for 1 minute, then repeat the process.

Pour the steak juices into the hot sauce, then remove the steak to a hot serving plate and pour over some of the sauce.

GAMMON, PINEAPPLE AND PEAS

This can be cooked either on a plate or dish or in a browning dish. A slightly browner appearance to the steak can be obtained by using the latter but the cooking time may be slightly longer. The pineapple is optional and a thick orange slice or two or three canned apricots can be substituted.

    1 × 100 g (4 oz) (approx.) round gammon steak
    Vegetable oil for brushing
    1 pineapple ring, fresh, frozen or canned
    3 heaped tablespoons frozen peas

    2 suitable sized undecorated dinner plates or browning
        dish with lid

Snip through the gammon rind at 65 mm (¼ in) intervals, then brush both sides of the steak lightly with the oil.

To cook on a plate, put the gammon in the centre of a suitable undecorated dinner plate, cover with a similar plate and cook on Full Power for 1 minute.

Carefully remove the top plate, and place the pineapple ring on the meat and surround the gammon with the peas.

Replace the covering plate and cook on Full Power for 2 minutes, then allow a standing time of 2 minutes before uncovering to serve.

To cook in a browning dish, preheat the unlidded dish in the microwave at Full Power for the maximum time recommended by the manufacturer.

When the browning dish is hot, quickly press the gammon steak on to the heated surface using a fish slice. Immediately turn the steak over, top with the pineapple ring, cover with the lid and cook for 1 minute.

Remove the lid and turn the gammon steak and pine-apple over, so that the pineapple is underneath. Add the frozen peas.

Replace the lid and cook for 1 minute or until the peas are cooked. Allow 2 minutes' standing time before removing the lid to serve.

HAM AND EGG PIE

Cooked potato is required in this recipe and if you have none available, the best thing to do is to cook the potato in its jacket, then peel and thinly slice it. It will take about 5 minutes in the microwave oven on Full Power.

    1 tablespoon vegetable oil
    1 small piece onion, peeled and chopped very finely
        until the juices run free
    1 level tablespoon flour

Salt
Freshly ground black pepper
¼ level teaspoon mustard powder
Dash Worcestershire sauce
7 tablespoons milk
175–200 g (6–7 oz) sliced cooked potato
1 hard-boiled egg, peeled and sliced (see page 211)
75 g (3 oz) chopped cooked pork, ham or luncheon
   meat, diced

0.55 litre (1 pint) jug
0.75 litre (1¼ pint) oval pie dish

Combine the oil and the onion in an 0.55 litre (1 pint) jug
and, without covering, cook on Full Power for 1 minute
to just soften the onion.

Stir in the flour, salt, pepper, mustard powder, Worcestershire sauce and lastly the milk. Cook, without covering, on Full Power for 1½–2 minutes or until the sauce
thickens. Stir with a fork once during and again at the
end of cooking time, making sure that the fork reaches
down to the bottom of the jug.

Arrange half the potato slices in the base of an 0.75
litre (1¼ pint) oval pie dish, cover with half the sauce,
then arrange the sliced egg on top. Now cover with the
diced meat followed by the remaining sauce and lastly
the potato.

Cook, without covering, on Full Power for 3–3½
minutes until hot, then if desired brown at a distance
from a hot grill – although this is not really necessary.

KIDNEYS, MUSHROOMS AND BACON IN RED
WINE SAUCE

This is a dish that goes well with boiled rice. Arrange
the rice in a border around the kidney mixture before

ing and add 1 extra minute to the heating time to ensure
that the rice will be hot.

2–3 lamb's kidneys, rinsed, halved and cored
50 g (2 oz) button mushrooms, thickly sliced or halved
2 rashers streaky bacon, trimmed and chopped
3 tablespoons medium red wine
Salt
Freshly ground black pepper
1 level teaspoon cornflour

0.75 litre (1¼ pint) casserole

Mix together the kidneys, mushrooms and bacon in an
0.75 litre (1¼ pint) casserole, sprinkle with 1 tablespoon
of the wine and season with salt and pepper. Cover with
the lid and cook on Full Power for 3½–5 minutes or until
the kidneys are cooked. Stir once during the cooking
period.

Transfer the kidney mixture to a warm plate using a
slotted spoon.

Blend the cornflour with the remaining 2 tablespoons
of the wine, then stir into the juices remaining in the
casserole. Cook, without covering, on Full Power for 1
minute, stirring the sauce once during this time.

Pour the thickened sauce over the kidneys, cover the
plate and reheat on Full Power for 1 minute.

LAMB CHOPS IN RATATOUILLE

Canned ratatouille is quite easy to obtain. The usual size
is 390g (13.5 oz). Use the whole can if you wish but
about half would do and you could save the rest to use
cold with a salad or add it to a can of tomato soup to
liven it up. There is a recipe for fresh ratatouille on page
165 or if you prefer you can use frozen ratatouille but this
must be partially thawed.

2 × 90–100 g (3–4 oz) lamb chops
300 ml (½ pint) ratatouille, canned, fresh or frozen

0.75 litre (1¼ pint) oval pie dish or plate

Trim the chops and place them in an 0.75 litre (1¼ pint) oval pie dish or plate, putting the thicker parts towards the ends or outside of the dish.

Pour the ratatouille over the chops so that they are completely covered and put any extra in the centre over the bones.

Cook, without covering, on Full Power for a minimum of 5 minutes and a maximum of 8 minutes depending upon which type of ratatouille you have used and the size of the chops. Test the chops after 5 minutes to see if they are cooked, and allow any additional cooking time necessary.

LIVER AND BACON KEBABS IN WINE SAUCE

Despite the title don't expect a large quantity of sauce in this recipe. There should be only just sufficient to coat the meat.

100 g (4 oz) liver (ox, pig, calf or lamb)
4 rashers streaky bacon
1 teaspoon vegetable oil
½ level teaspoon flour
3 tablespoons water
1 level tablespoon tomato ketchup
1 tablespoon red wine
Shake garlic powder
Salt
Freshly ground black pepper

4 wooden cocktail sticks
Shallow dish

Wash the liver and remove the tubes, then cut into eight pieces.

Remove the rind from the bacon. Lay the rashers on a board or work surface and stretch them with the back of a table knife. The bacon will become longer and thinner.

Cut each bacon rasher in half and wrap it round a piece of liver, then skewer two pieces of the wrapped liver on to each of 4 cocktail sticks. Place these on a shallow dish in a single layer and, without covering, cook on Full Power for 2 minutes. Remove the skewered meat from the dish.

Mix the remaining ingredients together in the dish with any residual liquid and cook, uncovered, on Full Power for 2–2½ minutes, stirring once during cooking. The sauce should now have thickened.

Remove the cocktail sticks from the meat (it is easier to do this by pushing the meat away with the rounded side of a fork), replace in the dish of sauce, turn the pieces over to coat the meat and reheat, without covering, on Full Power for 1 minute.

LIVER, MUSHROOMS AND TOMATO

100–150 g (4–5 oz) lamb's liver
1 tablespoon vegetable oil
8 button mushrooms (approx.)
1 tomato
Salt
Freshly ground black pepper

Small browning dish

Rinse and trim the liver, removing the skin and tubes, and pat dry with kitchen paper. Depending upon the thickness of the liver it can either be sliced or cooked in one piece.

Meanwhile preheat a small browning dish to the maximum recommended by the manufacturer (about 3 minutes). Add the oil and quickly press the liver on to the hot surface using a fish slice, then turn the liver over.

Arrange the mushrooms on one side or around the liver, cover the dish with the lid and cook on Full Power for 3 minutes or until the liver is only just cooked (test with a cocktail stick or sharp knife).

Halve the tomato and place cut-sides up on top of the liver, then replace the cover and cook on Full Power for 1 more minute or until the tomatoes are cooked. (If you overcook the tomatoes they will collapse).

Season just before serving.

MEAT BALLS IN CANNED CURRY SAUCE

Canned sauces come in a number of varieties and flavours. I have chosen curry for both the taste and colour. Red wine sauces are also good with meat balls, adding extra richness. Most canned sauces contain 300 g (10 oz) and I found that half this quantity was sufficient for the recipe. However, this recipe can be doubled in which case it will take 5–6 minutes to cook, but a larger dish will be needed and a round shape is more suitable.

1 slice bread, weighing about 40 g (1½ oz)
½ egg, beaten
1 very small onion or a piece weighing 25 g (1 oz), peeled
1 small piece carrot weighing about 25 g (1 oz)
100 g (4 oz) minced raw lean beef
Salt
Freshly ground black pepper
½ can ready-to-use curry sauce

0.75 litre (1¼ pint) oval pie dish

Remove the crust and put the bread in a mixing bowl, cover with the beaten egg, leave for a few minutes until the bread has soaked up all the egg. Mash with a fork.

Grate or very finely chop the onion and carrot and stir into the bread mixture, adding the barely seasoned mince. Shape into two balls.

Put the meat balls into an 0.75 litre (1¼ pint) oval pie dish and coat with the curry sauce. Cover the dish with greaseproof paper or vented cling film and cook on Full Power for 2 minutes.

Turn the meat balls over, then cook (covered) for a further 1½–2 minutes or until cooked. Leave to stand for 2 minutes before removing the cover.

Serve with freshly cooked tagliatelle which can, if desired, be cooked before the meat balls.

MINCE AND MUSHROOM CRUMBLE

Although many people prefer to use minced beef, it is now quite easy to obtain minced lamb or minced veal, so that you can ring the changes.

100 g (4 oz) lean raw minced beef
50 g (2 oz) button mushrooms, finely sliced
4 tablespoons beef stock
1 level teaspoon dried or fresh chopped chives
1 level teaspoon bottled fruity sauce (HP or similar)
Salt
Freshly ground black pepper
50 g (2 oz) flour
25 g (1 oz) butter or margarine
1 level teaspoon paprika
⅛ level teaspoon ground turmeric

0.75 litre (1¼ pint) oval pie dish

Mix the meat, mushrooms, stock, chives and sauce in an 0.75 litre (1¼ pint) oval pie dish and season with salt and pepper.

Put the flour into a mixing bowl and add the butter or margarine cut into small pieces, then rub with the fingertips until the mixture resembles fine crumbs. Stir in the paprika and turmeric.

Spoon the crumbed mixture over the meat and flatten with a knife or the back of a spoon. Cook, without covering, on Full Power for about 7 minutes or until the mince is cooked. Do not overcook or the meat will become very firm around the outside edge.

SAVOURY STUFFED PEPPERS

Red, yellow or black peppers can be used instead of the more common green pepper. Because they are sweeter it might be an interesting idea to omit the cheese and include a tablespoon of seedless raisins. Canned salmon or tuna fish can be substituted for the ham.

    1 small green pepper, rinsed and wiped dry
    1 thin slice bread, crusts removed
    1 egg, beaten
    25 g (1 oz) grated stale cheese
    15 g (½ oz) walnuts, finely chopped
    1 thin slice ham or salami, chopped, or 1 tablespoon
       cooked minced beef
    Salt
    Pepper
    1 level teaspoon tomato purée
    ½ level teaspoon cornflour

    0.55 litre (1 pint) bowl, measuring jug or casserole

To prepare the pepper, cut off and retain the stalk end and remove the seeds.

Break up the bread and mix with the egg, then when well soaked mash with a fork. Mix in the cheese, nuts and your chosen meat and season well with salt and pepper.

Stuff the mixture into the pepper and place it upright in an 0.55 litre (1 pint) bowl, jug or casserole. Put the pepper lid in position, then cover the jug with vented cling film and cook on Full Power for 3½–4½ minutes or until the pepper has changed to a more muted colour. Transfer the pepper to a heated serving plate.

Make up the liquid left in the jug to 60 ml (2 fl oz) with cold water. Stir in the tomato purée and cornflour. Season with salt and pepper and, without covering, cook on Full Power for 45–60 seconds or until the sauce begins to bubble.

Pour the sauce over the pepper and serve immediately.

STUFFED GREEN PEPPER

This is another of those versatile recipes which, provided you have an available pepper, can be concocted out of ingredients that you are likely to have in the cupboard. My tester liked the combination of the chicken and bacon flavours and because no left-over meat was to hand, a fresh pork chop was microwaved and the cooked flesh diced. Mushroom soup could be substituted for the chicken. Canned luncheon meat can take the place of left-overs, while instant mashed-potato powder requires no prior reconstituting.

1 large green pepper, well shaped
½ × 285 g (10 fl oz) can cream of chicken soup
2 rashers bacon, derinded and chopped
50 g (2 oz) left-over cooked meat, chopped

2 heaped tablespoons mashed potato, or 2 level
  tablespoons instant mashed-potato powder

1.95 litre (3½ pint) bowl
Shallow dish

Cut a slice from the stalk end of the pepper; rinse this
and retain. Remove and discard the seeds, pith and
membranes of the pepper. Rinse in cold water to remove
any remaining seeds.

Rinse the slice that you have removed and set aside.

Combine the soup, bacon and meat in a 1.95 litre (3½
pint) bowl and, without covering, cook on Full Power for
3 minutes to thicken the mixture slightly. Stir in the
mashed potato, then stuff the mixture into the pepper.

Stand the pepper in a suitable shallow dish and replace
the pepper lid. Cover with vented cling film. Cook on
Full Power for 3–4 minutes, or until the pepper is tender.

SWEET AND SOUR SPARE RIBS

An excellent easy recipe for anyone liking 'sweet and
sour'. There is very little meat on a spare rib and a
hungry person could probably cope with four.

4 pork spare ribs, total weight approximately 350 g
  (12 oz)
6 spring onions, trimmed and finely sliced
3 level tablespoons tomato purée
1 tablespoon fresh lemon juice
2 level tablespoons soft dark brown sugar
Dash Worcestershire sauce
½ level teaspoon French mustard
Salt
Freshly ground black pepper

1.25 litre (2¼ pint) casserole

Put the spare ribs into a 1.25 litre (2¼ pint) casserole dish, cover with the lid and cook on Full Power for 5 minutes.

Remove the ribs from the dish and drain away the fatty liquid. Using the same dish, mix together all the remaining ingredients and, without covering, cook on Full Power for 2 minutes, stirring after 1 minute.

Return the ribs to the dish and turn them so that they are completely coated with the sauce. Cook, without covering, on Full Power for 2 minutes or until the ribs are thoroughly reheated.

TANGY LEMON PORK CHOPS

A pork chop can lose as much as a quarter of its gross weight after it has been trimmed. Because of this it is impossible to give an exact cooking time, so it is advisable to test after 1 minute and then again every 30 seconds. Do not overcook the sauce under the impression that it will thicken further; extra cooking time will heat it too much and curdling will occur.

1 × 225 g (8 oz) pork chop, trimmed
15 g (½ oz) butter or margarine
1 tablespoon double cream
1 egg yolk
1–2 tablespoons medium dry white wine
1 wedge lemon, peeled, depipped and chopped
Salt and pepper
Suitable plate

0.55 litre (1 pint) bowl

Put the pork chop on a suitable plate, cover with grease-proof paper and cook on Full Power for 1 minute; turn the chop over and cook, still covered, for a further

30–60 seconds. Leave for a 2-minute standing time while preparing the sauce.

To prepare the sauce put the butter or margarine in an 0.55 litre (1 pint) bowl and heat without covering, on Full Power for 30 seconds, or until the butter is melted.

Stir in the cream, then add the egg yolk, wine and chopped lemon.

Reduce the setting to Defrost (30 per cent) and cook for 1 minute, beating every 20 seconds, until the sauce thickens slightly. Season to taste with salt and pepper.

Return the chop to the microwave oven for a 20-second boost on Full Power, then pour the sauce over the chop.

Serve with a jacket potato which could have been pre-cooked (reheating will then take between 2 and 3 minutes depending upon whether the potato has been refrigerated or is at room temperature).

CHICKEN À LA KING

Chicken à la King is usually made with cold cooked chicken but in this recipe I use a fresh chicken breast. The cooking time will be much the same.

20 g (¾ oz) butter or margarine
15 g (½ oz) flour
150 ml (¼ pint) milk
Salt
Pepper
100 g (4 oz) button mushrooms, sliced
1 × 150 g (5 oz) chicken breast, skinned and diced
2 teaspoons sherry
1 tablespoon double cream

1 litre (1¾ pint) bowl

First make the sauce. Put the butter into a 1 litre (1¾

pint) bowl and heat, without covering, on Full Power for
30 seconds or until the butter is melted.

Stir in the flour and cook for a further 20 seconds until
the mixture puffs up, then add the milk all at once and
whisk briefly with a wire whisk. Cook on Full Power for 1
minute, then whisk again. Cook for a further 30 seconds
and whisk more vigorously. Season sparingly with salt
and pepper.

Stir in the mushrooms, chicken and sherry and three-
quarters cover the bowl with cling film, leaving a gap so
that you can stir without dislodging the cling film. Cook
on Full Power for 3–4 minutes, stirring after each minute.

Adjust the seasoning and stir in the cream just before
serving.

CHICKEN BORDEAUX

Serve this dish with mashed potato or rice and sliced
carrots.

1 × 400 g (14 oz) chicken joint
About 1 tablespoon flour
Salt
Freshly ground black pepper
2 rashers streaky bacon, derinded and chopped
Shake garlic powder
1 celery stalk, finely sliced
2 level teaspoons chopped chives
4 tablespoons Bordeaux or medium red wine

Small browning dish with lid

Skin the chicken and dip it in the flour, shaking off the
surplus. Season lightly with salt and pepper.

Preheat a small browning dish to the maximum recommended by the manufacturer. Put the bacon in the

dish and cook, without covering, on Full Power for 1 minute.

Immediately add the chicken joint, rounded side down, and press the joint (using a fish slice or spoon) against the hot surface of the browning dish. Leave until the sizzling dies down, then add the garlic powder, celery and chives. Pour in the wine and turn the chicken joint over so that it is well coated.

Put the lid on the browning dish and cook on Full Power for 7–8 minutes or until the chicken is cooked.

Test the chicken with a sharp knife to make sure that there are no uncooked pink patches inside and give an additional minute if necessary. To be on the safe side allow a standing time of 3–4 minutes when the chicken will completely cook, due to the residual heat.

CHICKEN BREAST IN CREAMY SAUCE

Packaged golden crumbs are ideal for the coating but if you object strongly to using them, try well-crushed cornflakes instead. Serve with pre-cooked noodles, rice or mashed potatoes (reheat these before reheating the chicken with its cheese topping).

4 tablespoons double cream
1 bay leaf
1 sprig thyme
Squeeze lemon juice
Salt
Freshly ground black pepper
1 chicken breast, skinned and slightly flattened
½ beaten egg
2 level tablespoons golden crumbs
1 tablespoon vegetable oil
1 triangular portion processed cheese

0.55 litre (1 pint) jug
Shallow dish

Put the cream, bay leaf and thyme into an 0.55 litre (1 pint) jug and cook, without covering, on Full Power for 2 minutes until the cream boils rapidly. Remove the herbs and add the lemon juice, then season with salt and pepper. Cover and set aside.

Season the chicken with salt and pepper.

Put the beaten egg mixture on a small plate and spread out the crumbs on greaseproof paper.

Dip the chicken in the beaten egg, then place it in the centre of the crumbs and scoop the remaining crumbs on top. Press down well with a palette knife.

Put the oil into a suitable shallow dish that will comfortably accommodate the chicken piece and, without covering, heat on Full Power for 1 minute.

Lay the chicken on the hot oil 'best-looking' side down, cover with a small piece of non-stick paper and cook on Full Power for 1 minute. Turn the chicken over, replace the paper and cook for a further minute.

Remove the chicken, wipe the surplus oil from the dish and replace the chicken.

Unwrap the cheese portion and place it on top of the chicken and cook, without covering, on Full Power for 30 seconds. If serving with noodles, rice or mashed potatoes, reheat these before completely reheating the chicken. Smooth the softened cheese over the chicken breast, then pour the sauce on top.

Without covering, cook on Full Power for 30–60 seconds until reheated.

TURKEY, SWEETCORN AND ALMOND FRICASSÉE

175 g (6 oz) turkey fillet
Salt
Freshly ground black pepper
4 tablespoons sweet white wine
2 heaped tablespoons sweetcorn kernels, frozen or canned
2 level teaspoons soft margarine
2 level teaspoons flour
25 g (1 oz) toasted flaked almonds (see page 233)
2 tablespoons double cream
1 egg yolk

1 litre (1¾ pint) bowl

Season the turkey with salt and pepper, then cut into bite-sized pieces.

Combine the turkey in a 1 litre (1¾ pint) bowl with the wine and sweetcorn. Cover with vented cling film and cook on Full Power for 3 minutes, or until the turkey is cooked (the turkey flesh will appear white).

Blend the margarine and flour together in a small basin, remove the cling film from the bowl and add the paste in small quantities, beating in with a fork. Cook, without covering, on Full Power for 2–3 minutes, or until the sauce thickens. Adjust the seasoning if necessary and stir in half the nuts.

Blend together the cream and egg yolk, stir this into the turkey mixture and cook, without covering, on Full Power for 30–45 seconds. Do not overcook or the mixture may curdle.

Spoon the turkey fricassée on to a hot serving plate and sprinkle the remaining almonds on top.

CHEESE FONDUE

This is a simplified version of cheese fondue and uses Emmenthal cheese, but if you are really stuck you could use Cheddar. Left-over fondue freezes well and can be regenerated from frozen on the Defrost setting provided it is stirred frequently.

4 tablespoons dry white wine
50 g (2 oz) Emmenthal cheese, grated
Shake garlic powder
Freshly ground black pepper
Salt
1 teaspoon Kirsch
2 level teaspoons cornflour
Chunks of French bread for dipping

0.55 litre (1 pint) bowl
1 larger bowl to hold the boiling water

Put 3 tablespoons of the wine, the cheese, garlic powder and pepper into an 0.55 litre (1 pint) bowl and add a pinch of salt. Cook, without covering, on Full Power for 45–60 seconds, stirring twice with a fork during this time until the cheese is melted and floating around in the wine.

Blend the remaining wine, the Kirsch and cornflour in a small cup and pour into the cheese mixture. Stir and, without covering, continue cooking for 30–45 seconds, or until the mixture thickens and just starts to bubble but not rapidly boil.

While the fondue is cooking boil some water and pour a little into a bowl large enough to accommodate the cooking bowl. If you are not eating the fondue immediately (which of course you should) the bowl of fondue can happily sit in the very hot water while you are cutting the bread. This will help to prevent the fondue from over-thickening. However, if you don't want to bother with a second bowl, it doesn't matter. You can always put the fondue back in the microwave for a minute or two when it will thin out once more.

To eat, spear the bread with a fork and dunk into the creamy fondue.

CHEESE PUDDING

To vary this recipe, when mixing in the egg add 1 level tablespoon tomato ketchup or 1 slice of ham, finely chopped (or both) in which case the cooking time will need to be extended by 1–2 minutes.

If you are likely to use fresh breadcrumbs in several recipes, it is a good idea to grate a large quantity and store them in the freezer. The breadcrumbs will stay quite separate so there is no need to freeze them in small batches. A food processor or liquidizer can be used to grate the breadcrumbs as finely as desired.

150 ml (¼ pint) milk
6 level tablespoons fresh brown breadcrumbs
3 level tablespoons grated cheese
Pinch mustard powder
Salt
Freshly ground black pepper
1 egg, lightly beaten
Paprika ⎫
Freshly chopped parsley ⎬ optional

0.4 litre (¾ pint) oval pie dish.

Lightly grease the inside of an 0.4 litre (¾ pint) oval pie dish and pour in the milk. Cook, without covering, on Full Power for 1 minute, or until boiling. (You will probably see the oven door begin to steam up.)

Stir in the breadcrumbs, cheese, mustard powder, salt and pepper and then mix in the egg.

Reduce the setting to Defrost (30 per cent) and cook for 7½–8 minutes, or until the pudding is just set.

Sprinkle with paprika and parsley (if using) and serve at once.

DEVILLED MUSHROOMS

The microwave is champion at cooking mushrooms and this is an excellent and piquant recipe. Devilled mushrooms also make a good accompaniment for fish.

½ level teaspoon tomato purée
Dash Worcestershire sauce
⅛ level teaspoon French mustard
Pinch sugar
Salt
Freshly ground black pepper
75–100 g (3–4 oz) button mushrooms, halved
1 tablespoon single cream, or top of the milk

0.4 litre (¾ pint) pie dish

In an 0.4 litre (¾ pint) pie dish, blend together the tomato purée, Worcestershire sauce, mustard, sugar and a light seasoning of salt and pepper. Stir in the mushrooms until all are coated with the mixture.

Cover the dish with vented cling film and cook on Full Power for 1½–2 minutes.

Stir in the cream or top of the milk and, without covering, cook on Full Power for a further 15 seconds.

Serve hot with rice or cold with salad.

FIELD MUSHROOMS IN SOY AND SHERRY GRAVY

2 large open flat mushrooms
Freshly ground black pepper
1 teaspoon soy sauce
2 teaspoons sherry

Small shallow dish

Cut off the mushroom stalks level with the caps and roughly chop. Put the mushrooms, dark side up, side by side in a small shallow dish and place the chopped caps on top. Season with the pepper and sprinkle with the sauce and sherry.

Cover with vented cling film, a lid or an inverted plate and cook on Full Power for 3–4 minutes, or until the mushrooms are tender.

MUSHROOMS AND TOMATO IN MADEIRA SAUCE

Serve this dish accompanied with boiled rice, or use as a topping on jacket potatoes or freshly buttered toast. Extra sherry can be added to give a more pronounced flavour, and the quantity of flour fractionally increased to make the sauce thicker.

100 g (4 oz) button mushrooms, halved
1 large tomato, sliced
Salt
Freshly ground black pepper
2 bay leaves, or ⅛ level teaspoon bayleaf powder
1 teaspoon Madeira or sherry
1 teaspoon milk
1 teaspoon salad oil

1 level teaspoon flour
1 tablespoon cream (optional)

1 litre (1¾ pint) bowl

Put the mushrooms, tomato and a generous seasoning of salt and pepper in a 1 litre (1¾ pint) casserole or bowl and add the bay leaves or stir in the bay leaf powder. Sprinkle over the sherry and milk.

Cover with the lid or vented cling film and cook on Full Power for 3 minutes, or until the mushrooms soften. Meanwhile mix the oil and flour together to form a paste.

Uncover the casserole and, using a fork, whisk the flour paste into the mushroom mixture. Cook, without covering, on Full Power for 2 minutes, stirring after 1 minute. Remove the bay leaves if used and adjust the seasoning. Stir in the cream (if using).

POACHED SOUFFLETTE

This dish has a texture very similar to a soufflé. Although it tastes light it is, in fact, very filling and a side salad would probably be sufficient to serve with it for a light supper.

15 g (½ oz) butter
4 tablespoons milk
1 level tablespoon flour
1 level tablespoon Parmesan cheese, grated
Grated nutmeg
1 large egg, separated
Salt
Freshly ground black pepper
3 tablespoons chicken stock
2 level tablespoons frozen sweetcorn

For the topping:
3 tablespoons double cream
1 level teaspoon grated Parmesan cheese

1 litre (1¾ pint) bowl
0.4 litre (¾ pint) flameproof pie dish

Put the butter into a 1 litre (1¾ pint) bowl and heat, uncovered, for 30 seconds or until the butter is melted.

Stir in the milk and flour and cook on Full Power for 1–1¼ minutes until the sauce is thick, beating with a wire whisk every 30 seconds to prevent lumps forming.

Mix in the cheese, nutmeg and beaten egg yolk and season to taste with salt and pepper.

Put the stock and sweetcorn into an 0.4 litre (¾ pint) flameproof pie dish, cover with cling film and cook on Full Power for 2 minutes.

Using clean grease-free beaters whip the egg white until soft peaks form.

Fold the sauce into the egg white, then pour the mixture into the dish containing the stock and sweetcorn, leaving it to spread naturally.

Using a fresh piece of cling film cover the dish, leaving a vent. Reduce the setting to Defrost (30 per cent) and cook for 4–5 minutes, or until the soufflette is just set.

Spoon the cream over the top and sprinkle with the Parmesan cheese. Brown under the grill.

Note: If the pie dish is not flameproof, but is made of glass or pottery, it will probably be safe to use provided that it is placed no nearer than 15 cm (6 in) from the grill element.

SAVOURY RAREBIT

A variation on the Welsh Rarebit theme, the mixture has
a 'bite' to it. Savoury Rarebit makes a substantial meal
but it is also palatable cold if two slices are too much.

Small piece onion, peeled and very finely chopped
50 g (2 oz) grated Cheddar cheese
1 egg
¼ level teaspoon mustard powder
1 tablespoon milk
1 level teaspoon bottled fruit sauce
2 slices bread
Butter

0.5 litre (1 pint) bowl

Switch on the grill ready to cook the toast.

In an 0.5 litre (1 pint) bowl, beat together thoroughly
the onion, cheese, egg, mustard powder, milk and sauce
and, without covering, cook on Full Power for 30 seconds.
Beat again, then cook (still uncovered) for a further 30
seconds. Beat once more and, if the mixture has not
thickened, cook for a further 30 seconds.

While the sauce is cooking, toast the bread. Quickly
butter the toast, pour the sauce over the top and brown
both slices under the grill.

SPINACH OMELETTE

Use freshly cooked spinach leaves or frozen leaf or
chopped spinach for this recipe. Remember to drain the
spinach before mixing with the other ingredients.

2 eggs
Salt
Freshly ground black pepper

Pinch nutmeg
100 g (4 oz) cooked spinach
Grated Parmesan cheese

Well-greased 21.5 cm (8½ in] round pie dish

Well grease a 21.5 cm (8 ½ in) round pie dish.

Separate the eggs and beat the whites until soft peaks form. Beat the yolks together with the salt, pepper and nutmeg and stir in the spinach.

Fold the spinach mixture into the beaten egg whites, then pour into the prepared dish. Cook, without covering, on Medium (50 per cent) for 4–5 minutes until just set but not shrunken.

While the omelette is cooking prepare a hot grill, then when the omelette is ready sprinkle it with Parmesan cheese and brown under the grill.

Lift the omelette on to a plate folding it in half, brown-side uppermost. This will leave space for any vegetables or salad that you are serving with it.

Note: The omelette can also be cooked on Full Power – this will take about 2½ minutes but is a less reliable method of cooking.

STUFFED JACKET POTATO

This is very much cheaper to prepare at home than having a take-away from the local 'Spud House'.

1 freshly cooked jacket potato
Chosen filling

Either split the cooked potato in half or cut a lid from the top lengthways. Scoop out the potato flesh and mix with the chosen filling.

Filling suggestions:
(a) 2 drained sardines, mashed
(b) 2 level tablespoons grated Edam cheese; salt and pepper
(c) 2 level tablespoons cream cheese and 1 level table-spoon chopped olives; salt and pepper.
(d) 1 teaspoon tomato purée; pinch dried basil; 1 level tablespoon grated Parmesan cheese; ½ slice sweet cured ham, diced.
(e) 1 rasher bacon, cooked and diced; 1 lightly scrambled egg.
(f) 1 tablespoon chopped fresh parsley; small knob butter; salt and pepper.
(g) 1 tablespoon chopped salted peanuts; knob butter; 1 tablespoon milk.

COQUILLES ST JACQUES SAVOYARD

Coquilles St Jacques Savoyard is a rich and special dish which you can have as a starter or as a main course with brown bread and butter and a crisp green salad. Fresh or frozen scallops may be used.

Frozen scallops must be thawed first (which will only take about 10 minutes in cold water). They may be defrosted in the microwave if it has a very low setting (such as 10 per cent) when they will be ready in 3 minutes. If the lowest setting is Defrost (30 per cent) allow about 3 minutes but stir frequently.

Fresh scallops must be washed in cold water and any grit removed. The fishmonger will take the scallop off the shell and will certainly give you the shell if you ask for it. They are quite expensive to purchase.

4 tablespoons dry white wine
1 tablespoon water

1 slice onion
1 clove
1 bouquet garni
2 peppercorns
Salt
Freshly ground black pepper
1 slice lemon
3 large scallops, fresh or frozen and thawed
1 level tablespoon Dijon mustard
Pinch dry mustard powder
1 egg yolk
¼ level teaspoon tomato purée
2 capers, finely chopped
1 level teaspoon freshly chopped parsley, or ¼
    teaspoon dried parsley
20 g (2 oz) unsalted butter
Lemon slice to garnish

1.25 litre (2¼ pint) casserole

Put the wine, water, onion, clove, bouquet garni, peppercorns, salt, freshly ground black pepper and lemon slice
into a 1.25 litre (2¼ pint) casserole and cook, uncovered,
on Full Power for 5 minutes.

Add the scallops, cover with the lid and cook on Full
Power for 1–1½ minutes, or until the scallops are opaque.
(Do not overcook or they will shrivel.) Leave in the
covered casserole to keep warm.

In a small bowl mix together the mustards, egg yolk,
tomato purée, capers and parsley and add 2 tablespoons
of the liquid that the scallops have been cooked in.

Put the butter into a slightly larger bowl and heat,
without covering, on Full Power for 30 seconds or until
melted. Beat in the mustard mixture using a wire whisk.
Reduce the power to Defrost (30 per cent) and cook for
1–2 minutes, beating every 30 seconds, until the sauce

thickens slightly. (The sauce curdles rapidly if overheated, so when you see the mixture bubbling around the edges – which is the first sign of the curdling process – beat vigorously, mixing the outside edge of the mixture with the remainder in the centre, and all should be well.)

Transfer the scallops to a shell or small ramekin dish, pour the hot sauce over the top and decorate with a lemon slice.

The dish may be reheated on Defrost (30 per cent) for about 2 minutes.

PRAWN, SALMON AND TUNA QUICHE

Vary the filling to suit yourself. It is perfectly all right to use all prawns or all tuna, or a mixture of the two.

For the pastry:
75 g (3 oz) flour
40 g (1½ oz) soft margarine
About 2 tablespoons milk

For the filling:
2 eggs
7 tablespoons milk
25 g (1 oz) cooked, shelled prawns, thawed if necessary
25 g (1 oz) smoked salmon, shredded
25 g (1 oz) flaked canned tuna fish

0.4 litre (¾ pint) oval pie dish
1 litre (1¾ pint) jug

To make the pastry, put the flour into a mixing bowl, rub in the margarine, add sufficient milk to mix to a very soft dough, gather into a ball and put into an 0.4 litre (¾ pint) pie dish. Using your fingers press the pastry well into the sides and base. Refrigerate for 30 minutes.

Put a piece of greaseproof paper into the pie dish over the pastry so that it comes well up the sides; fill with baking beans (raw rice and lentils are suitable but ceramic beans are best as they get hot and help to cook the pastry). Cook, without covering, on Full Power for 3 minutes. Remove the beans and greaseproof paper and cook for a further minute.

Beat the eggs and milk together in a 1 litre (1¾ pint) jug, stir in the prawns and cook, without covering, on Full Power for 1 minute. Stir, then test to see if the prawns are thawed and when they are, cook for a further minute or until the mixture begins to thicken and to coagulate around the edges.

Stir in the remaining fish, then pour the mixture into the pastry case.

Reduce the setting to Defrost (30 per cent) and cook, without covering, for 10 minutes or until only the centre remains slightly wobbly. The filling will set further as it cools. If after cooking for the specified time the quiche is very runny in the centre, leave to stand for 20-30 minutes, then cook on Defrost (30 per cent) for a further 5–10 minutes. Serve cold.

PRAWN AND TARRAGON PILAU

The pink prawns give an attractive rosy colour to this delicious easy-to-cook dish.

15 g (½ oz) butter or margarine
50 g (2 oz) easy-cook long grain rice
1 level tablespoon chopped mixed nuts
1 level tablespoon sultanas
50 g (2 oz) shelled cooked prawns, fresh or frozen
¼ level teaspoon dried tarragon
Salt

Freshly ground black pepper
300 ml (½ pint) hot chicken stock

1.25 litre (2¼ pint) casserole

Put the butter into a 1.25 litre (2¼ pint) casserole dish
and heat, without covering, on Full Power for 30 seconds,
or until the butter has melted.

Stir in the rice and nuts and cook, without covering,
for 2 minutes. Stir in all the remaining ingredients and
cook, without covering, for 12 minutes, stirring once
during cooking. At the end of this time stir immediately,
then put the lid on the casserole and leave to stand for 5
minutes before serving.

BACON AND ONION FLAN

I use 100 per cent wholemeal flour to make the pastry for
this flan and this should add a touch of fibre to your
meal. The pastry case may also be made with white flour
and will need less milk.

For the pastry:
75 g (3 oz) wholemeal flour
40 g (1½ oz) soft margarine
About 2 tablespoons milk

For the filling:
1 small onion, peeled and very finely chopped
1 rasher bacon, derinded and finely chopped
1 teaspoon vegetable oil
1 egg
6 tablespoons milk
Salt
Freshly ground black pepper

0.4 litre (¾ pint) pie dish
0.55 litre (1 pint) jug

To make the pastry, put the flour into a mixing bowl and mix in the margarine using a round-bladed knife. Add sufficient milk to form a soft dough.

Lightly grease an 0.4 litre (¾ pint) pie dish and press the dough into the base and sides. Refrigerate for 30 minutes.

Put a large piece of greaseproof or non-stick paper on top of the pastry and fill with baking beans. Cook, without covering, on Full Power for 3 minutes, then remove the paper and beans and continue cooking, uncovered, for a further minute.

For the filling, first mix the onion, bacon and oil together and spread in the bottom of the pastry case.

In an 0.55 litre (1 pint) jug beat together the egg, milk and a light seasoning of salt and pepper and cook, without covering, on Full Power for 1 minute. Pour the egg mixture over the onion and bacon mixture. Reduce the setting to Defrost (30 per cent) and cook, without covering, for about 10 minutes until the outside of the filling is set and the centre almost set. Cover with cling film and leave to stand for 10 minutes, then remove the cling film and put the tart in a cool place until quite cold.

BROWN BEEF AND ONION CASSEROLE

The larger supermarket chains now sell fresh ready-cubed beef suitable for goulash or bourguignonne. One of the drawbacks is that you cannot always buy a small enough quantity for one person. However, any surplus can be frozen for use another time. Use a good quality sweetish wine to obtain the best flavour. Serve with mashed potato, boiled rice or noodles.

175 g (6 oz) cubed beef (approx.)
25 g (1 oz) butter or margarine

⅛ level teaspoon sugar
2 level tablespoons flour
150 ml (¼ pint) full-bodied red wine
3–4 tablespoons water
Salt
Freshly ground black pepper
12 bottled pearl or small pickled onions

Small browning dish with lid

Put the beef cubes into a small browning dish, cover with the lid and cook on Full Power for 1 minute. Remove the beef.

Put the butter and sugar into the unrinsed browning dish and cook, without covering, on Full Power for 3 minutes or until a nice deep brown deposit occurs. Immediately toss in the beef, turning it over to coat well. Cover and cook on Full Power for 1 minute.

Stir in the flour, then add the wine, water, seasoning and the onions. Replace the lid and cook on Full Power for 5–6 minutes, stirring once during cooking.

CARROT, PARSNIP AND BACON HOT POT

This tastes much better than it sounds and is best eaten piping hot. Although the casserole can be cooked in advance, it tends to thicken during standing time, so extra water or stock should be stirred in before reheating.

3 rashers back bacon
2 medium (about 100 g (4 oz)) carrots
1 medium young parsnip
1 small onion
Pinch dried thyme
Salt
Freshly ground black pepper

225 ml (8 fl oz) water
1 level teaspoon cornflour

1.25 litre (2¼ pint) casserole

Remove the rind and chop the bacon. Peel the vegetables and cut into thin slices.

Put the bacon into a 1.25 (2¼ pint) casserole and cook, without covering, on Full Power for 2 minutes.

Remove the bacon with a slotted spoon and drain away the fat.

Put the carrots, parsnip, onion, herbs, salt, pepper and water in the casserole, stir, cover with the lid and cook on Full Power for 11–14 minutes, or until the vegetables are tender. (Take care when removing the lid before the next stage, as the hot steam may burn your hands.)

Blend the cornflour with 2 tablespoons of cold water, then stir into the vegetables, adding the reserved bacon.

Stir thoroughly then cook, without covering, on Full Power for a further 2 minutes.

CIDER RABBIT

Although this is for rabbit lovers, turkey or chicken can be successfully substituted.

1 rasher streaky bacon, rind and bones removed
2 tablespoons salad oil
1 small onion, peeled and finely chopped
1 level tablespoon flour
Salt
Freshly ground black pepper
225 g (8 oz) rabbit, cubed
1 level tablespoon Dijon mustard
¼ level teaspoon bay leaf powder

Pinch dried thyme
4 tablespoons cider

1.25 litre (2¼ pint) casserole

Snip the bacon into tiny pieces with scissors and put into
a 1.25 litre (2¼ pint) casserole, stirring in 1 tablespoon
of the oil. Mix in the onion and cook, without covering,
on Full Power for 2 minutes.

Mix the flour with the salt and pepper, either on a
sheet of greaseproof paper or in a clean polythene bag,
and toss the rabbit in the mixture. Stir the rabbit cubes
into the casserole and cook, without covering, on Full
Power for 2 minutes. Stir, then cook for a further 1
minute.

Drain away any excess fat and stir in any seasoned
flour that remains.

Mix in the mustard, bay leaf powder, thyme and then
the cider.

Cover with the lid, reduce the setting to Medium (50
per cent), and cook for 12–16 minutes. Leave to stand
for 5 minutes before serving.

Note: This dish improves if rapidly cooled and refrigerated
overnight to be thoroughly reheated on Medium (50 per
cent) the next day. Do not be under the impression that
further cooking will additionally tenderize the rabbit – it
doesn't, it only makes it tougher.

LAMB RAGÔUT

A sort of Middle Eastern dish.

15 g (½ oz) butter
Pinch sugar
Pinch ground mixed spice

Shake garlic powder
1 small onion, peeled and very finely chopped
25 g (1 oz) pine kernels
175 g (6 oz) cubed lamb, trimmed if necessary
1 level tablespoon flour
1 × 227 g (8 oz) can tomatoes
Squeeze lemon juice
Salt
Freshly ground black pepper

1.25 litre (2¼ pint) casserole

Put the butter into a 1.25 litre (2¼ pint) casserole and cook, without covering, on Full Power for 30 seconds or until melted.

Stir in the sugar and spice, then add the garlic powder, onion and nuts and cook, without covering, on Full Power for 2 minutes. Stir, then cook, still uncovered, for a further 2 minutes.

Toss or dip the lamb cubes in the flour and stir the meat, but not any surplus flour, into the casserole. Cook, without covering, on Full Power for 3 minutes, stirring the meat once, until it is sealed.

Stir in the canned tomatoes with their juice, the lemon juice and season with salt and pepper.

Place the lid on the casserole and cook on Full Power for about 6 minutes. Stir once during the cooking time if you remember, it's not frantically important.

MOUSSAKA

We have eaten this freshly cooked, reheated from the refrigerator and even from frozen. Although the dish was best freshly cooked, it was still most acceptable when reheated. If you wish, you can use a whole egg for the sauce but it will be thicker and firmer.

1 × 285 g (10 oz) aubergine
Salt
1 small onion, peeled and very finely chopped
2 teaspoons vegetable oil
1 small clove garlic, peeled and crushed
75 g (3 oz) minced lean raw beef
2 level tablespoons tomato purée
2 tablespoons water
Salt
Freshly ground black pepper
¼ level teaspoon dried marjoram
½ beaten egg
4 tablespoons soured cream
1 level tablespoon grated Parmesan
1 level tablespoon grated Cheddar cheese

Suitable plate
1.1 litre (2 pint) bowl
0.7 litre (1¼ pint) flameproof pie dish

Peel and slice the aubergine thinly, spread out on a suitable plate, sprinkle very lightly with salt, then cover with vented cling film and cook on Full Power for 2 minutes. Strain.

In a 1.1 litre (2 pint) bowl, mix together the onion, oil and garlic and cook, without covering, on Full Power for 3 minutes. Stir in the beef and cook for 1½–2 minutes, stirring once during cooking. The meat should be cooked by now but if not, then cook for a further minute. Spoon away any surplus fat. Stir in the tomato purée, water, salt and pepper to taste and the marjoram.

Form alternate layers of aubergine and meat sauce in an 0.7 litre (1¼ pint) flameproof pie dish, finishing with aubergine. Cover with vented cling film and cook on Full Power for 4 minutes.

Meanwhile mix together the egg, cream and Parmesan.

Carefully remove the cling film from the pie dish and pour the egg sauce over the mixture. Reduce the setting to Defrost (30 per cent) and cook, uncovered, for 5 minutes or until the topping begins to set.

Sprinkle with the Cheddar cheese and brown at a distance from a hot grill.

PORK, KIDNEY BEAN AND APPLE DINNER

A meal in itself which is highly nutritious and also tastes good. Although the chop is pale, the flavour and texture is excellent and if you wish to garnish to improve the appearance, then sprinkle with a little paprika and freshly chopped parsley.

2 level tablespoons easy-cook long-grain rice
6 tablespoons water
Salt
Freshly ground black pepper
Pinch ground cloves
50 g (2 oz) canned kidney beans, rinsed
1 × 100 g (4 oz) dessert apple
1 × 225 g (8 oz) pork chop, trimmed
Freshly chopped parsley and paprika to garnish (optional)

1.25 litre (2¼ pint) casserole

Combine the rice and water in a 1.25 litre (2¼ pint) casserole, season generously with salt and pepper, add the ground cloves, then stir in the kidney beans.

Peel, core and slice the apple and add to the mixture, then place the chop on top.

Cover with the casserole lid and cook on Full Power for 9–10 minutes, or until the chop is just cooked and the apples are soft. Leave to stand covered for 5 minutes to enable the chop to finish cooking without becoming tough and to ensure that the rice is tender.

SAUSAGE RISOTTO

2 beef or pork sausages
4 level tablespoons easy-cook long-grain rice
Salt
Pinch ground cardamom
Pinch ground turmeric
1 level tablespoon frozen peas
1 level tablespoon sweetcorn kernels
¼ green pepper, diced
150 ml (¼ pint) water

1.25 litre (2¼ pint) casserole

Put the sausages into a 1.25 litre (2¼ pint) casserole dish and cook, without covering, on Full Power for 45 seconds. Remove and slice the sausages.

Stir the rice and all the other ingredients into the dish, cover with the lid and cook on Full Power for 6 minutes. Uncover, stir in the sausages, replace the lid and cook for a further 6 minutes. Stir once, then leave to stand, covered, for 2–3 minutes before serving.

SHEPHERD'S PIE

It is usual to use left-over roast lamb or beef to make Shepherd's or Cottage Pie but the meat must be minced. Not many people have a mincer nowadays, but the food processor does an excellent chopping job. Of course left-overs may not be available but you can use fresh mince. First cook it separately in a small bowl in the microwave, then drain off the fat. Shorten the cooking time when heating the finished dish. Approximately 175 g (6 oz) of fresh mince is equivalent to 100 g (4 oz) of cooked mince.

Unless you have left-over mashed potato ready you will first have to prepare some for topping the dish. To do this either cook one large potato in its jacket, then scoop out and mash the contents or prepare one large portion of reconstituted instant potato.

1 small onion, peeled and very finely chopped
2 teaspoons vegetable oil
2 level teaspoons flour
¼ beef stock cube, crumbled (Oxo gives a good
   flavour)
5 tablespoons hot water
100 g (4 oz) cooked minced beef or lamb (approx.)
Salt
Freshly ground black pepper
About 200 g (7 oz) mashed potato

0.4 litre (¾ pint) oval pie dish

Mix the onion and oil together in an 0.4 litre (¾ pint) oval pie dish and cook, without covering, on Full Power for 2 minutes.

Mix in the flour and cook for a further 3 minutes, stirring frequently until the flour browns.

Stir in the stock cube and hot water, then add the mince and season to taste with salt and pepper.

Smooth the top of the mixture, then pipe or spread the mashed potato on top and ridge the surface with a fork.

Cook, without covering, on Full Power for 4–7 minutes until the meat is thoroughly hot, when the internal temperature of the meat will be 80°C (175°F). The cooking time will depend upon the temperature of the meat at the start.

Place at a distance under a hot grill until the potato has browned.

SPRING LAMB CHOPS

I used frozen chops for this recipe because I wanted to see if I could achieve as satisfactory a texture as when cooking fresh or thawed chops. The result was a pleasant surprise. Of course you don't *have* to use frozen chops and thawed or fresh chops will cook in about half the time.

A browning dish achieves better results but an ordinary microwave-suitable casserole can be substituted. Use any cooked or canned vegetables but take care when reheating small young canned carrots; the dish must be covered, in case any of them explode.

2 × 125 g (4½ oz) frozen lamb chops
Salt
Freshly ground black pepper
Few drops gravy browning, gravy powder or beef
    extract (i.e. Bovril)
About 8 spring onions, topped, tailed and finely sliced
1 serving of canned or cooked carrots, peas, beans,
    parsnips or potatoes

Browning dish with lid

Place the chops side by side in an unheated small browning dish; cover with the lid and cook on Full Power for 3 minutes. Turn the chops over and cook, covered, for a further 5–6 minutes or until they are just cooked. Drain away any surplus fat.

Remove the chops from the dish, season them with salt and pepper, then brush on both sides with a little gravy browning.

Drain away any surplus fat from the dish and return it, uncovered, to the microwave and heat on Full Power for 1 minute. Immediately add the spring onions, stir thoroughly and cook, without covering, for 1 minute, stirring once during that time.

Without wasting any time, place the chops side by side on top of the sizzling onions, pressing them well down to achieve browning. Turn the chops over, add the vegetables around the side of the dish, cover with the lid and cook on Full Power for 1 minute.

Transfer to a warmed dinner plate with a slotted spoon.

CHICKEN KIEV

Use either packeted golden breadcrumbs or crushed cornflakes for coating the chicken pieces. If using the latter, you will need about 3 heaped tablespoons of cornflakes. These can be crushed by placing them in a polythene bag and squeezing, or simply by breaking them up with a fork on a large plate.

1 chicken breast, skinned
25 g (1 oz) butter
1 level teaspoon freshly chopped parsley
Salt
Freshly ground black pepper
1 beaten egg
1–2 level tablespoons golden breadcrumbs or crushed cornflakes
1 tablespoon oil

Browning dish

Beat the chicken breast with the back of a cleaver or rolling pin until it is flat. (The easiest way to do this is by sandwiching the chicken breast between two large sheets of cling film so that fragments of the meat do not break off and stick to the rolling pin.)

Mix together the butter, parsley, salt and pepper and form into an oblong shape in the centre of the chicken meat. Fold one edge of the chicken over to enclose the parsley butter completely, fold in the two sides and, finally, roll the chicken up rather like a *Chinese* spring roll. Chill in the freezer for 15 minutes.

Put the beaten egg into a shallow dish and the crumbs on a sheet of greaseproof paper, then dip the chicken first in the egg and then into the crumbs. Shake off the surplus crumbs, then dip the chicken roll in the egg and crumbs once again, pressing the crumbs into the sides with a palette knife.

Preheat a browning dish to the maximum recommended by the manufacturer and add the oil. Quickly put the chicken on to the hot surface of the browning dish and then turn the roll over quickly to brown the other side.

Cook, without covering, on Full Power for 1 minute, then turn the chicken over and cook (still uncovered) on Full Power for 1 further minute.

Leave to stand for 2 minutes before serving.

Note: Take care when cutting through the chicken as the butter tends to spurt out. Serve with Lyonnaise potatoes or chips with peas or salad.

CHICKEN MUSSOORI

Mild curry-coated chicken cooked on a bed of flavoured onion which ideally should be served with boiled rice. The rice can be cooked in advance to be reheated either separately or with the chicken on the serving plate.

Chicken joints vary in size and may be leg or wing so that it is impossible to give an exact cooking time. It is better to thaw frozen chicken before cooking, otherwise the skin is practically impossible to remove.

1 chicken joint
1½ level teaspoons plain flour
½ level teaspoon curry powder
½ level teaspoon ground cumin
¼ level teaspoon ground turmeric
Pinch chilli compound powder
⅛ level teaspoon paprika
Pinch salt
Pinch freshly ground black pepper
Shake garlic powder
1 teaspoon vegetable oil
1 small onion, peeled and finely chopped
2 tomatoes, quartered
1 level teaspoon desiccated coconut
1 tablespoon mango chutney
2 tablespoons water

1.25 litre (2¼ pint) round casserole

Rinse and skin the chicken. Mix together the flour, curry powder, ground cumin, ground turmeric, chilli compound powder, paprika, salt, pepper and garlic powder in a medium-sized polythene bag, add the chicken and shake the bag gently until the chicken is thoroughly coated with the powder. Remove the chicken from the bag and prick deeply with a fork.

In a 1.25 litre (2¼ pint) round casserole, mix together the oil and onion, cover with the lid and cook on Full Power for 3 minutes.

Stir in the tomatoes, desiccated coconut, mango chutney and the water. Add the coated chicken piece smooth side down, replace the casserole lid and cook on Full Power for 5 minutes. Turn the chicken over and continue cooking, covered, for a further 5 minutes or until the chicken is tender.

Serve with boiled rice or pitta bread which needs only 20 seconds in the microwave to warm it through.

CHICKEN AND OLIVE CASSEROLE

A casserole which is cooked without fat or thickening so will appeal to those who dislike rich sauces.

1 × 275 g (10 oz) chicken joint
Salt
Freshly ground black pepper
1 × 100 ml (4 fl oz) bottle tomato cocktail
1 small onion, peeled and finely sliced
6 stoned olives, sliced
Squeeze lemon or fresh lime juice
1 small potato, peeled and diced

1.25 litre (2¼ pint) casserole

Remove the skin and season the chicken with salt and pepper. Place in a 1.25 litre (2¼ pint) casserole with all the other ingredients. Cover with the lid and cook on Full Power for 10 minutes.

Remove the lid carefully and inspect to make sure that the casserole juices have not dried up too much (if so, then stir in 1–2 tablespoons water). Replace the lid and cook on Full Power for a further 5 minutes or until the chicken is fully cooked.

To serve appetizingly, pile the vegetables on top of the cooked chicken.

CAULIFLOWER CHEESE AND CHIVES

4 tablespoons water
Salt
225 g (8 oz) prepared cauliflower florets
15 g (½ oz) butter or margarine
150 ml (¼ pint) cold milk
2 level teaspoons cornflour
1 level tablespoon chopped chives
2 rounded tablespoons grated cheese
Freshly ground black pepper
2–3 tablespoons brown crumbs (optional) (see page 229)

1.25 litre (2¼ pint) casserole

Put the water into a 1.25 litre (2¼ pint) casserole with a little salt. Add the cauliflower florets and spread around the casserole. Cover with the lid and cook on Full Power for 5–6 minutes, or until the cauliflower is just tender.

Remove the cauliflower with a slotted spoon. (You can put it on the casserole lid to save extra washing up.) Stir the butter into the liquid in the dish and when it is melted, stir in 2 tablespoons of the cold milk and then blend in the cornflour.

Add the remainder of the milk and the chives and cook, without covering, on Full Power for 5 minutes, stirring two or three times during cooking.

Mix in the cheese (the texture will now be rather like thick cream). Season with pepper.

Replace the cauliflower in the dish and coat with the sauce. Cover with the lid and cook on Full Power for 1 minute, or until the cauliflower is reheated.

Sprinkle with browned crumbs if desired (these can be cooked in advance or just before preparing the cauliflower).

MACARONI CHEESE

50 g (2 oz) macaroni can absorb as much as 300 ml (½ pint) water, so that if you add more macaroni to the sauce, you must also increase the quantity of hot water and allow additional cooking time.

2 tablespoons vegetable oil
2 level tablespoons flour
150 ml (¼ pint) milk
Salt
White pepper
Pinch mustard powder
300 ml (½ pint) hot water
50 g (2 oz) quick-cooking macaroni
50 g (2 oz) Cheddar cheese, grated

1.25 litre (2¼ pint) bowl

Put the oil into a 1.25 litre (2¼ pint) bowl and stir in the flour, then thoroughly mix in the milk using a wire whisk.

Cook, without covering, on Full Power for 1 minute, stir with the whisk, then continue cooking for a further minute, whisking once during cooking and then more vigorously afterwards. You should now have a smooth sauce of coating consistency.

Season the mixture with salt and pepper and add the mustard powder, then blend in the hot water.

Cook, without covering, on Full Power for 1–2 minutes or until you see the sauce beginning to boil, then stir in the macaroni.

Three-quarters cover the bowl with cling film and cook on Full Power for 10–12 minutes, stirring occasionally through the vent.

When the macaroni is tender, stir in the cheese. Cook on Full Power for a further minute, then cover the bowl completely and leave to stand for 2–3 minutes before serving.

STUFFED AUBERGINE

After cooking the stuffing, it should be packed into the aubergine skin. In the unlikely event of the skin collapsing altogether, then do the reheating in the pie dish.

1 medium aubergine, about 275 g (10 oz)
1 small onion, peeled and finely chopped
1 level tablespoon butter
1 level tablespoon tomato purée
Shake garlic powder
¼ level teaspoon bayleaf powder
25 g (1 oz) grated or finely chopped hazelnuts
100 g (4 oz) cooked minced meat or chicken, or 1 small
    can tuna fish, drained
Salt
Freshly ground black pepper
1 tomato

0.75 litre (1¼ pint) pie dish

Wash the aubergine, trim away the stalk end, then prick all over. Put in an 0.75 litre (1¼ pint) pie dish and cook, without covering, on Full Power for 5 minutes.

Remove a thin slice along the top of the aubergine, scoop out and reserve the flesh. Set aside the shell.

Drain the liquid from the dish and put in the onion and butter. Cook, without covering, on Full Power for 3 minutes, then stir in the well-chopped aubergine flesh, the tomato purée, garlic powder, bayleaf powder, nuts and your choice of meat, chicken or fish.

Season with salt and pepper, then either pack the

mixture into the aubergine shell and put on a plate, or leave in the dish, discarding the shell.

Slice the tomato and arrange on top of the mixture, then cook, without covering, for 3 minutes or until the filling is hot.

BEEF IN BROWN ALE

This is a dish that improves by being made in advance and stored overnight in the refrigerator or for a few days in the freezer. During this time and through the reheating process, the meat becomes rather more tender. The gravy is on the thin side which goes well with the cooked sliced potato.

175 g (6 oz) braising steak, cut into bite-sized pieces
1 tablespoon lemon juice
1 level tablespoon tomato purée
Salt
Freshly ground black pepper
1 large potato about 250 g (9 oz), peeled and sliced
    thickly
2 medium carrots, peeled and sliced
2 bay leaves
300 ml (½ pint) brown ale
Dash Worcestershire sauce
2 level teaspoons clear honey

1.1 litre (2 pint) casserole

Pierce the steak cubes, then place in a 1.1 litre (2 pint) casserole with the lemon juice and tomato purée and mix well. Cover with the lid and set aside for 30 minutes.

Add the remaining ingredients to the casserole. Cover with the lid, leaving a small gap for steam to escape, and cook on Full Power for 10 minutes, stirring once during cooking. Stir, then replace the lid, again leaving a small gap and continue cooking as before for a further 10 minutes, or until the vegetables are tender. Now cover completely with the lid and leave to stand for 5 minutes before serving.

CARIBBEAN CURRY

    1 small onion, peeled and finely chopped
    1 tablespoon vegetable oil
    ½ level teaspoon mustard seed
    1 level tablespoon Garam Masala (curry powder)
    175–200 g (6–7 oz) trimmed lamb, cubed
    1 tablespoon fresh lemon juice
    1 rounded tablespoon mango chutney
    Few grains red food-colouring powder
    1 rounded tablespoon desiccated coconut
    Salt
    Freshly ground black pepper
    150 ml (¼ pint) water
    1 ripe banana

    1.25 litre (2¼ pint) casserole

In a 1.25 litre (2¼ pint) casserole, mix together the onion and oil and cook, without covering, on Full Power for 3 minutes, stirring at least once during cooking.

Add the mustard seed and Garam Masala and cook for 1 minute to give the spices a chance to develop their flavour.

Add the lamb, lemon juice, mango chutney, food colouring, coconut, salt and pepper and cook, without covering, on Full Power for 5 minutes.

Stir in the water. Peel and cut the banana into four pieces and put these in the centre of the casserole, pushing the pieces of meat towards the outside.

Cover with the lid, reduce the power to Defrost (30 per cent) and cook for 25–35 minutes, stirring once during cooking.

Serve with boiled rice which can be reheated on Full Power for a minute or two on a plate or in the lid of the casserole. The curry will remain hot for about 5 minutes.

CHILLI CON CARNE

100 g (4 oz) raw lean minced beef
½ small green pepper, seeded and finely chopped
1 small onion, peeled and finely chopped
¼ clove garlic, crushed, or shake garlic powder
2 tomatoes, peeled and chopped
2 level tablespoons tomato purée
½ level teaspoon chilli compound powder or pinch ground chillis
Salt
Freshly ground black pepper
1 level teaspoon bottled fruit sauce (HP or similar)
3 heaped tablespoons canned kidney beans, rinsed

1.25 litre (2¼ pint) casserole

In a 1.25 litre (2¼ pint) casserole, combine all the ingredients except the kidney beans. When well mixed, fold in the kidney beans.

Cover with the lid and cook on Defrost (30 per cent) for 30 minutes. This is a dish which should cook well without needing to be stirred.

Serve in taco shells or with boiled rice.

HUNGARIAN GOULASH

This is a meat dish that improves if cooked rapidly and then refrigerated for several hours before reheating. If you do cook in advance, add the yogurt and cornflour just before reheating.

1 tablespoon vegetable oil
1 small onion, peeled and finely chopped
½ small green pepper, seeded and diced
Salt
Freshly ground black pepper
100 g (4 oz) cubed beef or veal
1 level teaspoon sweet paprika
1 level tablespoon tomato purée
Pinch caraway seeds (optional)
1 tomato, quartered
1 small potato, peeled and diced
5 tablespoons water
4 tablespoons natural yogurt
2 level teaspoons cornflour

1 medium browning dish with lid

Preheat a medium unlidded browning dish to the maximum recommended by the manufacturer, then quickly stir in the oil, onion and diced pepper. Cook, without covering, on Full Power for 2 minutes. Stir, then cook for a further 1–2 minutes or until the vegetables are cooked but not burning.

While the vegetables are cooking, season the meat. Toss it into the sizzling vegetables and cook, without covering, on Full Power for 1 minute.

Stir in the paprika, tomato purée, caraway seeds, quartered tomato, diced potato and the water. Cover with the lid and cook on Full Power for 5 minutes. Stir and, reducing the setting to Defrost (30 per cent) cook, covered, for a further 15 minutes.

Blend together the yogurt and cornflour and pour into the hot goulash. Cook, without covering, on Defrost (30 per cent) for 5 minutes, stirring halfway through cooking.

LAMB HOTPOT

This is quite a substantial meal on its own. You can add more potato if you wish and possibly extend the cooking time by another 5–10 minutes.

    1 level tablespoon flour
    Salt
    Freshly ground black pepper
    Shake garlic powder
    Pinch sugar
    175–225 g (6–8 oz) trimmed lamb cut into bite-sized
        pieces
    1 teaspoon vinegar
    6 tablespoons water or stock
    1 medium-sized red pepper, seeded and cut into 1.5 cm
        (¾ in) dice
    2 tomatoes, quartered
    1 medium onion, peeled and quartered
    1 medium potato, peeled and quartered
    ¼ level teaspoon dried lemon thyme or other herbs

    1.25 litre (2¼ pint) casserole

In a 1.25 litre (2¼ pint) casserole, mix together the flour, a generous seasoning of salt and pepper, garlic powder and sugar, then add the pieces of lamb and toss so that they are well coated. Sprinkle with vinegar.

Add the water or stock, cover with the lid and cook on Full Power for 5 minutes. (If during cooking you see the liquid boiling up, move the lid slightly to one side to leave a gap for the steam to escape.) Push the meat towards the sides of the dish and put the remaining ingredients in the centre. Replace the cover completely and cook on Defrost (30 per cent) for 25–30 minutes, stirring once about three-quarters of the way through the cooking period.

MINCED BEEF STROGANOFF

¼ onion, peeled and very finely chopped
100 g (4 oz) raw minced lean beef
1 level teaspoon flour
Shake garlic powder
1 level tablespoon tomato purée
1 level teaspoon French mustard
½ teaspoon fresh lemon juice
50 g (2 oz) mushrooms, finely sliced
5 tablespoons water
¼ beef stock cube, crumbled
Salt
Freshly ground black pepper
4 tablespoons soured cream
175 g (6 oz) cooked rice

0.75 litre (1¼ pint) casserole

In an 0.75 litre (1¼ pint) casserole, mix together the onion and meat and cook, without covering, on Full Power for 3 minutes. Drain away the surplus fat.

Sprinkle the flour over the meat, then stir in the garlic powder, tomato purée, mustard, lemon juice, mushrooms, water and stock cube. Season to taste with salt and pepper but do not over-salt as the stock cube will tend to be salty.

Cover with the lid and cook on Defrost (30 per cent) for 20 minutes, stirring half-way through cooking.

Stir in the cream and set aside, covered, while reheating the rice.

STEAK AND KIDNEY PUDDING

For the filling:
50 g (2 oz) ox kidney
100 g (4 oz) braising steak
1 small onion, peeled and grated
Knob of butter
2 level teaspoons flour
¼ beef stock cube
Salt
Freshly ground black pepper
4 tablespoons hot water

For the suet pastry:
100 g (4 oz) plain flour
1 level teaspoon baking powder
½ level teaspoon salt
50 g (2 oz) shredded suet
4–5 tablespoons cold water
Extra flour

1 litre (1¾ pint) bowl
0.55 litre (1 pint) bowl, greased

First make the filling. Trim, rinse and very finely chop the kidney. Finely dice the steak. If you prefer, you can chop the whole lot in the food processor or put the meat through a mincer. Whichever method you choose, because of the comparatively short cooking time you must make sure that the steak is chopped up quite small. If you are using the food processor or the mincer, you could process the onion at the same time, otherwise peel and grate the onion or chop very finely.

Put the butter in a 1 litre (1¾ pint) bowl and heat, without covering, on Full Power for about 30 seconds or until it is melted.

Stir in the flour, then add all the other filling ingredients, making sure that the stock cube is well crumbled.

Stir once, then three-quarters cover the top of the bowl with cling film, leaving a gap so that you can stir through it during cooking. Cook the filling for between 5 and 7 minutes so that the meat is cooked, stirring once during this period. Test a morsel of the beef but bear in mind that it will undergo additional cooking when it is in its pastry case.

While the meat is cooking you can prepare the suet pastry. First, well grease an 0.55 litre (1 pint) basin and set aside. Sift the flour, baking powder and salt into a bowl, then stir in the suet. Gently mix in sufficient water to form a soft dough. (If the dough is too stiff, you will have difficulty in moulding it and it will dry out and become hard during cooking.)

Shape the dough into a ball on a very lightly floured surface, then cut out one-quarter. Set the latter aside, covering it to prevent drying out. Reshape the remaining pastry into a ball, then roll or press firmly into a circle measuring about 30 cm (12 in) across, or more than twice the diameter of the top of the prepared basin.

Insert the rolled-out dough into the greased basin, easing it so that the dough reaches to the rim. Spoon the filling into the basin. Shape the reserved pastry into a lid and place on top of the meat. Dampen the inside edge of the protruding pastry lining and fold this over the lid to form a tight seal.

Slit the lid once with a sharp knife, then cover the

basin loosely with cling film so that when the pudding rises it will have room to expand. Put the pudding in the centre of the microwave oven and cook for 15 minutes on Defrost (30 per cent).

Pull back one corner of the cling film and leave the pudding to stand for 5 minutes before serving. If you are going to turn the pudding out, first make sure that it is loose. A table knife drawn round between the pastry and the basin, using a light sawing motion, should do the trick.

Note: This recipe is really quite easy to prepare and is not as fiddly as you might think. The quantity is the smallest that I would recommend but might well do for two servings. If you find you have a surplus then rapidly cool, cover and freeze for future use.

Thaw, covered, in the microwave oven set on Full Power for 1 minute. Reduce the setting to Defrost (30 per cent) and continue microwaving until thoroughly reheated – about 5 minutes.

CHICKEN IN GREEN PEPPER SAUCE

The sauce will be creamier if the dish is served fresh but it also freezes satisfactorily. To reheat, place the frozen food in a dish, cover and set on Defrost, stirring once as soon as the chicken begins to thaw and once before serving. It will take 7–10 minutes.

    1 × 300–350 g (10–12 oz) chicken joint
    300 ml (½ pint) water
    ½ small green pepper, seeded and diced
    1 level tablespoon plain flour
    Salt

Freshly ground black pepper
1 egg yolk

1 litre (1¾ pint) bowl

Put the chicken joint into a 1 litre (1¾ pint) bowl and add the water. Cover with vented cling film and cook on Full Power for 15 minutes. Remove the chicken with a slotted spoon and discard the skin and bones. Cut up the flesh into bite-sized pieces.

Strain the liquid into a measuring jug. Put one tablespoon of the fat that rises to the surface back into the cooking bowl, then skim away and discard the remainder.

If necessary make up the liquid in the jug to 250 ml (8 fl oz) with water.

Stir the diced pepper into the fat in the bowl, cover with vented cling film and cook on Full Power for 1 minute.

Remove the cling film, stir in the flour, season with salt and pepper and stir in all but four tablespoons of the liquid in the jug. Cook, uncovered, on Full Power for 4 minutes or until the sauce thickens slightly.

Add the chicken and cook, uncovered, on Full Power for 2 minutes or until the chicken is hot.

Blend the egg yolk with the reserved four tablespoons of liquid, then stir this into the chicken and sauce. Reduce the setting to Defrost (30 per cent) and cook, without covering, for 3 minutes, which time should be sufficient to just thicken the sauce.

Serve with mashed potato, boiled rice or spaghetti.

CHICKEN AND WHITE WINE CASSEROLE

The chicken remains pale but is balanced by the delicate green of the celery and beans which can be spooned on top for serving.

1 × 300–350 g (10–12 oz) chicken joint, skinned
100 g (4 oz) mushrooms, sliced
2 tablespoons (50 g (2 oz)) frozen freshly sliced green
   beans
½ celery stalk, finely sliced
1 small onion, peeled and very finely chopped
½ level teaspoon dried tarragon
½ level teaspoon dried parsley
4 tablespoons medium white wine
Salt
Freshly ground black pepper
2 level teaspoons dried potato powder

1.25 litre (2¼ pint) round casserole

Put all the ingredients except the potato powder into a
1.25 litre (2¼ pint) round casserole. Turn the chicken
over once or twice to coat it with the liquid, then cover
with the lid and cook on Full Power for 5 minutes.

Stir in the potato powder, reduce the setting to Defrost
(30 per cent) replace the casserole lid and cook for a
further 15–20 minutes or until the chicken is opaque
throughout (check by piercing the chicken with a sharp
knife).

Serve with additional mashed potatoes.

CHRISTMAS ROAST DUCK

Even if you are on your own you can still enjoy an
exciting Christmas dinner. Buy the tenderest juiciest duck
portion that you can obtain. If it is frozen, allow it to
completely thaw before cooking.

1 duck portion weighing about 400 g (14 oz)
Salt
Pepper

1 level tablespoon clear honey
6 chestnuts
Pinch cornflour

21.5 cm (8½ in) round pie dish or casserole
1 undecorated saucer

Put the duck portion on an upturned undecorated saucer in 21.5cm (8½ in) round pie dish or casserole and season with salt and pepper. Cover with a lid or split roast-a-bag and cook on Defrost (30 per cent) for 20–25 minutes until the duck is tender. Remove the dish from the microwave.

Slash the chestnuts on a board with a sharp knife, then put into the microwave and cook on Full Power for 30–45 seconds until the chestnuts feel very hot to the touch. Remove them carefully from the microwave, then peel, skin and quarter as soon as possible.

Remove the duck from the dish, take out the saucer, then spoon away the surplus fat. Stir the honey into the juices, mix in the cornflour and stir in the chestnuts.

Remove the skin and place the duck portion in the sauce. Cover with vented cling film or a lid and reheat on Full Power for 2 minutes. Serve with sprouts and potatoes.

KICHKIRI

A mixture of lentils, rice and spices which is traditionally served with a sliced-egg topping. Non-vegetarians may add chopped ham or serve on a slice of ham. A slice of cooked roast beef can be reheated with the rice but must be removed from the dish before stirring in the yogurt. Whether or not the lentils and rice need pre-rinsing depends on the instructions on the packet.

Ordinary long-grain rice may be used but extra water is then likely to be required.

1 teaspoon salad oil
1 slice onion, finely chopped
Shake garlic powder
Shake turmeric
Shake ground cloves
Shake ground cinnamon
2 whole cardomom pods
Generous 150 ml (¼ pint) hot water
2 level tablespoons easy-cook long-grain rice
2 level tablespoons red lentils
Salt
Pepper
Generous tablespoon plain yogurt
1 hard-boiled egg, sliced

0.55 litre (1 pint) casserole

Put the oil, onion, garlic and spices into an 0.55 litre (1 pint) casserole. Cover and cook on Full Power for 2 minutes.

Stir in the water, rice and lentils and cook, without covering, on Full Power for 3 minutes or until boiling.

Season with salt and pepper, then cover. Reduce the setting to Defrost (30 per cent) and cook for 15 minutes until the rice and lentils are tender.

Stir in the yogurt, then arrange the hard-boiled egg slices on top.

SPINACH AND CASHEW NUT QUICHE

An oval pie dish may seem a strange shape for a quiche but this is the shape to give the best results for meals for one.

For the pastry:
75 g (3 oz) flour
40 g (1½ oz) soft margarine
1–2 tablespoons milk

For the filling:
250 g (8.8 oz) pack frozen chopped spinach
2 level tablespoons tomato purée
1 egg, beaten
15 g (½ oz) cashew nuts, chopped
Salt
Freshly ground black pepper

0.4 litre (¾ pint) oval pie dish
0.55 litre (1 pint) bowl

To make the pastry, put the flour in a mixing bowl, rub in the margarine and blend in the milk. Shape into a soft ball, then place in an 0.4 litre (¾ pint) oval pie dish and, using the backs of your fingers, press the pastry into the sides and base of the dish. Refrigerate for 30 minutes.

Put a piece of greaseproof paper into the pastry in the dish and fill with baking beans. (The best kind to use are the ceramic beans because these attract the microwaves, become hot and help to cook the pastry.) Cook, without covering, on Full Power for 3 minutes, then remove the greaseproof paper and beans, and cook the pastry for a further minute.

Put the spinach into an 0.55 litre (1 pint) bowl, cover with a suitable plate and cook on Full Power for 7–9 minutes, removing the plate and breaking up the frozen block with a fork two or three times during cooking.

Into the cooked spinach, mix the tomato purée, then the beaten egg and half the nuts. Mix very thoroughly to ensure an even blend and then season to taste with salt and pepper.

Pour the filling into the pastry case, sprinkle with the remaining cashew nuts and cook, without covering, on Full Power for 9–10 minutes or until the colour of the filling darkens.

Serve warm or leave to cool in the pie dish. When the pastry is cold, it is easy to lift out in one piece but if you only wish to eat half, then leave the remainder in the dish. Should you wish to reheat, microwave on Full Power for about 1 minute.

Vegetables, Rice and Pasta

Vegetables cooked in small portions retain many more of their vitamins than when cooked in large quantities. The colour stays bright, the texture is tender but not mushy – altogether there is no better way of cooking vegetables than in the microwave oven. Like everything else some care is needed but the rules are few.

Vegetables with a high water content need little or no additional water – these include spinach, mushrooms, courgettes, marrow and tomato halves. All these, except the tomatoes, should be cooked entirely covered or covered and vented. Season these vegetables after cooking rather than sprinkling salt over them before cooking.

Root vegetables, which include carrots and parsnips, must be peeled or scraped and cut into even-sized pieces, either rounds or chunks. Put about half a cupful of water into a casserole and stir in salt to taste. Add the vegetables, cover with the lid or vented cling film and cook on Full Power for 6–8 minutes for a 100 g (4 oz) portion, which before peeling might weigh nearer 200 g (8 oz), although 175 g (6 oz) fresh vegetables should be sufficient.

Roasting bags are useful cooking containers for vegetables. Put the vegetables and the required amount of water into the bag, draw the edges together and slip a large elastic band over the top, leaving a finger-thick aperture.

Roasting bags are not cheap and are re-usable. To drain without destroying the bag hold carefully with oven gloves and gradually lift the bag until the cooking water can flow freely through the aperture. Put the bag on a plate or dish, snip off the elastic band, take out the potatoes and serve. If you wish to keep the vegetables hot for a few minutes after draining, fold the bag down over the vegetables, tucking the edges under. The heat will be retained for quite a time.

Old potatoes when peeled and cut up need no special care, but new potatoes if overcooked will be spongy inside. I discovered two satisfactory methods of cooking new potatoes (first having washed, but not peeled, them).

The first method is to put them in a roasting bag with a cupful of water. Cook on Full Power, allowing 5–6 minutes for 225 g (8 oz). Half-way through cooking joggle the bag, using oven gloves, so that any potatoes shielded by others can be repositioned – this is not as difficult as it sounds. Season with salt and pepper after cooking.

Any dirt which might have adhered to the potatoes will dissolve in the cooking water. If this is the case, rinse the potatoes in boiling water after draining.

The second method for cooking new potatoes is in a casserole, adding sufficient water only to cover. Stir the salt into the water before adding the potatoes and cook, covered, with the larger potatoes positioned towards the outside of the casserole and the smaller ones in the centre. Push them around with a spoon once during cooking.

Prick, score or top and tail vegetables enclosed in a skin according to their variety.

Tufted vegetables on thick stalks, including cauliflower and broccoli, require their florets to be broken off, discarding any dry tough stalks. Cut up the thin stalks and mix together with the florettes in a small casserole. Add salted water and cook covered.

Leeks require plenty of water to cook and the addition of a knob of butter greatly improves the flavour. You can cook them whole, halved or sliced. If you are slicing the leeks it is better to do so diagonally, Chinese fashion. Cook in a small casserole with a narrow diameter and covered with a lid or vented cling film. Sometimes they boil over but it is better to cook completely covered and wipe up the mess rather than balance the lid leaving a gap to prevent boiling over.

Cook frozen vegetables on Full Power from frozen, i.e. do *not* defrost first. Put pouches of frozen vegetables in a dish, then slash through the top of the pouch and cook without adding water. If cooking frozen vegetables taken from a large pack, add 2–3 tablespoons water mixed with ¼–½ teaspoon salt. Cook, covered with a lid or vented cling film, on Full Power. Cooking times will be fractionally less than those for fresh vegetables. The reason for this is that although frozen vegetables are already partly cooked, they start off very cold while fresh vegetables, although raw, are less so.

The chart at the end of this section lists packs of frozen vegetables in the smallest sizes available in a local shop. Most contain 225–250 g (8–8.8 oz) which means that they either have to be cooked all at once in the pack or in the quantity you require. In the latter case, if you have freezer space you may well save money by buying bigger packs. Peas are the most popular frozen vegetable and can be obtained in smaller packs as can beans. A spoonful or two will cook on the dinner plate (provided the plate is covered) alongside other, cooked, ingredients which are being reheated, and will hardly add to the cooking time.

Frozen vegetables requiring similar cooking times can be cooked together in the same dish and will remain in their own section of the dish provided they are not stirred. You can of course put them in separate small dishes and cook them side by side, but the dishes must be given a

Fresh Vegetables Requiring Varied Attention

Vegetable	Quantity	Water	Salt	Dish	Technique	Cooking time	Standing time
Artichoke	1	4 tbsps	Nil	0.55 litre (1 pint) bowl	Upright, covered.	5–6 minutes	2 minutes
Asparagus	225 g (8 oz)	4 tbsps	Yes plus knob butter	0.55 litre (1 pint) jug	Upright, upside-down, unsealed, in tented roasting bag.	6–7 minutes	2 minutes
Aubergine	225 g (8 oz)	4 tbsps	Optional	Oval pie dish	Sliced or halved, covered.	4–5 minutes	3 minutes for halves. Nil for slices
Beetroot	2 medium	150 ml (¼ pint)	Nil	1 litre (1¾ pint) bowl	Whole unpeeled, covered.	4–5 minutes	5 minutes
Corn on the Cob	1 medium	Nil	Nil	Oval pie dish	Remove silk. Cook, uncovered, in husk. Turn over half-way through cooking.	3–4 minutes	2 minutes
Fennel	175 g (6 oz)	4 tbsps	Yes	0.55 litre (1 pint) casserole	Rinse and halve. Slice thinly. Cook covered.	5–7 minutes	Nil
Onions	100 g (4 oz)	Only if sliced	Yes	Casserole or bowl	Cook, covered.	2–3 minutes	Nil

half-turn once during cooking or, alternatively, stirred. When cooked this way a little extra time will be needed.

Dried vegetable flakes, particularly onion and celery, are handy for flavouring and they need no prior attention if the particular soup or casserole has more than 5 minutes' cooking time. Dried vegetables should be soaked in the cooking liquid for half an hour before commencing cooking.

The lone diner may resort to the use of cans. With these, you can heat the contents either drained or in their liquor. Put them in a covered dish to heat. If they are still in their liquor, drain before serving. Can sizes vary and if you are only requiring half the contents, then heat that amount and store the remainder, covered, in the refrigerator. A single serving of drained canned vegetables will take about 1 minute to heat.

Cooking Frozen Vegetables You will see from the chart below that timings are very similar – single portions will take just over half the time stated. As a rule I allow about 3–4 minutes for vegetables cooked in water and 2½–3½ minutes for high-water-content vegetables cooked without added water.

Vegetable	Packet Size	Time	Comments
Asparagus spears	200 g (7 oz)	6–9 minutes	Separate and reposition after 3 minutes.
Beans, green, sliced	225 g (8 oz)	6–8 minutes	
Beans, cut or whole	100 g (4 oz)	4–5 minutes	
Beans, haricot vert	300 g (10 oz)	7–9 minutes	
Broad beans (podded)	225 g (8 oz)	7–8 minutes	Add more water, stir once during cooking and do not overcook or they will become tough.

Vegetable	Packet Size	Time	Comments
Broccoli spears	225 g (8 oz)	6–9 minutes	Separate and reposition after 3 minutes.
Brussels sprouts	225 g (8 oz)	6–8 minutes	Sprouts continue cooking after removing from the microwave unless the lid is immediately taken off. Do not overcook or they become spongy.
Cabbage, chopped	450 g (1 lb)	8–10 minutes	Stir once during cooking.
Cauliflower florets	175 g (6 oz)	5–8 minutes	No water needed; stir once during cooking.
Carrots	225 g (8 oz)	6–7 minutes	
Corn on the cob	1 cob 2 cobs	3–4 minutes 6–7 minutes	Do not add water, cover with greaseproof paper (not cling film which makes the kernels too soft).
Peas	114 g (4½ oz) 225 g (8 oz)	3–4 minutes 5–6 minutes	
Petit pois	225 g (8 oz)	4–5 minutes	
Spinach, chopped	150 g (5 oz)	6–7 minutes	Do not add water.
Spinach, whole leaf	250 g (8 oz)	6–7 minutes	Break up block as soon as possible, stir once when thawed.
Spinach, pellets (available in large packs only)	Single serving	3–4 minutes	
Sweetcorn	250 g (8 oz)	4–6 minutes	
Swedes and turnips	Single serving	3–4 minutes	Mash with butter and season after cooking.

Packs of frozen mixed vegetables are available, with combinations of cauliflower, peas and spinach; peas and baby carrots; and sweetcorn, peas and carrots. Cook similarly to peas.

THE RECIPES

Baked Tomatoes
Beetroot
Beetroot Salad
Braised Celery
Broad Beans
Brown Rice
Brussels Sprouts (Fresh)
Courgettes
Creamy Mushroom Filling
Jacket Potatoes
Mashed Potato
Mushrooms à la Grecque
Oven Chips
Pasta

Plain Cooked Cabbage
Potato Salad
Potato Skins
Ratatouille
Reconstituting Instant Potato
   Powder
Rice – Traditional and
   Modern
Scalloped Potatoes Gratinée
Spinach – Fresh and Frozen
Super Swedes
Tagliatelle Nests
Vegetable Marrow

BAKED TOMATOES

Tomatoes collapse suddenly in the microwave and covering aggravates the situation. Choose large firm tomatoes for this method of cooking and preferably set the cooker on Defrost (30 per cent). When cooking tomatoes on a plate with other items such as bacon or sausages, add the tomatoes towards the end of the cooking period.

1 to 2 large firm tomatoes

Suitable plate or dish

Cut the tomatoes in half crosswise and put them cut-side up and spaced out on a suitable plate.

Cook, without covering, on Full Power for about 5–10 seconds per half or for 30 seconds per half on Defrost (30 per cent).

Remove each tomato half as soon as it is cooked.

BEETROOT

Beetroot is a wonderful salad vegetable and is particularly appetizing when cooked in the microwave oven. A couple of small beetroot can be cooked very quickly by this method and if you like them on the firm side, 6 or 7 minutes will do. If you like your beetroot softer, then they will take about 10 minutes.

2 × 75 g (3 oz) raw unpeeled beetroot
150 ml (¼ pint) hot water

1.25 litre (2¼ pint) casserole

Put the beetroot into a 1.25 litre (¼ pint) casserole, add the hot water, then cover with the lid or cling film and cook on Full Power for 6–10 minutes. Leave to stand for about 10 minutes before removing the cover and draining the beetroot. Skin hot or cold and use as required.

BEETROOT SALAD

1 slightly undercooked beetroot, peeled
1 level tablespoon mayonnaise
1 teaspoon French dressing
Freshly chopped parsley

Peel the beetroot and grate coarsely or cut into very thin strips. Mix the mayonnaise and French dressing together, then fold in the beetroot. Sprinkle with chopped parsley.

BRAISED CELERY

1 small onion, peeled and finely chopped
15 g (½ oz) butter
4 celery stalks, cut into 2.5 cm (1 in) lengths
Salt

Freshly ground black pepper
Pinch grated nutmeg

0.75 litre (1¼ pint) casserole

Put the onion and butter into an 0.75 (1¼ pint) casserole dish and cook, without covering, on Full Power for 1 minute or until the butter has melted.

Stir, then continue cooking, uncovered, for a further 2 minutes.

Mix the celery into the onion mixture and season with salt, pepper and nutmeg. Cover with the lid and cook for 2 minutes.

Add 4 tablespoons water, replace the lid once more and cook for 6–8 minutes, stirring once during cooking.

BROAD BEANS

Except when they are very young and small, broad beans must be podded before cooking. (You have to buy about 450 g (1 lb) to yield roughly 75 g (6 oz) of beans.) The beans from old tough pods may have tough skins but this is rare when you buy beans in season. 450 g (1 lb) broad beans before podding should be sufficient for a generous portion as a vegetable, with a few beans left over that you can put into salads.

175 g (6 oz) podded broad beans
300–450 ml (½–¾ pint) hot water

1.25 litre (2¼ pint) casserole

Put the beans into a 1.25 litre (2¼ pint) casserole and add the water. (Do not add salt because salt tends to toughen the skins.)

Cover tightly and cook on Full Power for 7–10 minutes. Remove the lid, test a single bean and, if necessary, continue cooking. Drain well before serving.

BROWN RICE

4 tablespoons (50 g (2 oz)) brown rice
225 ml (8 fl oz) boiling water
¼ teaspoon salt

1.25 litre (2¼ pint) casserole

Combine the rice, water and salt in a 1.25 litre (2¼ pint) casserole dish, cover with a lid and cook on Full Power for 12 minutes or until the rice is just tender. Stir once, replace the lid immediately and leave to stand for 5 minutes before serving.

At the end of the standing time, inspect the rice. If there is too much liquid remaining, cook on Full Power in the uncovered casserole for 5 minutes or until the liquid has evaporated. On the other hand, if the liquid has all been absorbed but the rice is still too firm, add 2–3 tablespoons water, replace the cover and cook for a further 4–5 minutes on Full Power.

BRUSSELS SPROUTS (FRESH)

175 g (6 oz) firm even-sized fresh sprouts
4 tablespoons water
Salt

0.4 litre (¾ pint) pie dish

Rinse and trim the sprouts (which will now weigh about 125 g (4½ oz)) and put them into an 0.4 litre (¾ pint) pie dish with the salted water.

Cover with the lid or vented cling film and cook on Full Power for 5–6 minutes, stirring half-way through cooking. Since cling film is difficult to reposition, you may prefer to use a lidded casserole.

COURGETTES

These really do cook well in the microwave and do not need any additional water. Provided you buy firm courgettes they will not be bitter, so if you are able to feel them when you buy them, don't purchase any that are the slightest bit soft. You can cook them whole, sliced, halved or cut into matchsticks. If you are able to choose even-sized courgettes, then cook them whole; if you find that you have one large and two small, it is much better to cut them up.

    225 g (8 oz) courgettes
    Grated nutmeg
    Freshly ground black pepper
    Butter
    Salt

    0.4 litre (¾ pint) pie dish

Wash, top and tail the courgettes and, if desired, cut them up. Place them in an 0.4 litre (¾ pint) pie dish. Whole or split courgettes should be put in one even layer, sliced courgettes can be piled up.

Sprinkle the courgettes with grated nutmeg and pepper, add a dab or two of butter but only the *tiniest* sprinkling of salt, if any, or the courgettes will dry up and shrivel.

Cover with the lid or vented cling film and cook on Full Power for 2 minutes. Check to see if the courgettes are almost tender (if you have covered with cling film you will be able to test the courgettes through the cling film with the handle of a fork). If the vegetables are not nearly cooked, replace the cover and cook on Full Power for a further minute, bearing in mind that the courgettes will continue to cook after leaving the microwave oven as they retain quite a lot of heat. Overcooked courgettes become spongy.

CREAMY MUSHROOM FILLING

You can use this as a sauce; as a filling for pancakes or vol-au-vent cases; as a stuffing for tomatoes; to accompany spaghetti; or as a lasagne filling.

Mushrooms are very low in calories – about 4 calories per 25 g (1 oz), so this could be made into a slimmer's recipe by using skimmed rather than full cream milk.

The filling thickens as it cools, so if it is being reheated you should stir in an extra tablespoon or so of milk or water.

1 level tablespoon soft margarine
2 level tablespoons flour
150 ml (¼ pint) milk
Salt
Freshly ground black pepper
About 50 g (2 oz) button mushrooms

Put the margarine, flour and milk into a 1 litre (1¾ pint) bowl and stir throughly (the margarine may not completely blend). Cook, without covering, on Full Power for 1 minute, then beat thoroughly with a wire whisk.

Continue cooking, without covering, for a further minute, whisking once during and once after cooking. Season with salt and pepper.

Chop the mushrooms as finely as you like, then stir them into the sauce. Cook, without covering, on Full Power for between 2 and 4 minutes, stirring with the whisk every minute until the mushrooms are tender.

If you are not using the filling at once, cover with cling film to prevent a skin forming. It will keep for 1–2 days in the refrigerator. Although it does not freeze particularly well, you can do so and then regenerate in the microwave on Full Power for 4–5 minutes, whisking thoroughly and frequently, adding a little extra milk if necessary.

JACKET POTATOES

If you buy large potatoes for baking you can serve them either in the traditional jacket-potato fashion or you can scoop out the centres as soon as they are cooked and use as mashed potato. If you are in a hurry, you will find that two small potatoes will cook more quickly than one large potato. You can, if you wish, cook two, three or four jacket potatoes at one time and store them in the refrigerator to reheat the next day. I have even frozen whole jacket potatoes and found them to be very palatable when defrosted and heated through.

When cooking potatoes in this way, at the end of the cooking period you must make sure that they are ready to eat before you cut them. As soon as they are split, much of the heat and moisture that was trapped inside the skins is lost and then it is very difficult to continue cooking them in the microwave open. Should this happen, clamp the top and bottom of the potato back together, wrap in cling film and then continue cooking.

Over-cooking will cause the potato flesh to become very dry and spongy and so you need to be able to judge when they are ready – if a good squeeze, without actually breaking the skin, is possible then they should be just right. The cooked potatoes will keep hot for at least 30 minutes if you wrap them in a clean teacloth or cup them in the ends of oven gloves. Don't wrap them in foil to keep hot; the skins will become very soft due to the condensation that builds up inside the foil covering.

One jacket potato weighing about 200 g (7 oz) will take about 4 minutes on Full Power, two similarly-sized potatoes will take between 6 and 8 minutes, while three potatoes will take 9–10 minutes. Having pricked the potato(es), place them on a sheet of kitchen paper. If you are cooking one, place it in the centre of the oven. If you are cooking more than one, arrange them in a circle well spaced out. Half-way through cooking turn the potatoes over – this is particularly important if the potatoes are taller rather than longer.

It goes without saying that the potatoes must be scrubbed and pricked before cooking, but it does not matter if you have not dried them very well.

Because of their starchy nature the liquid that comes out through the pricked holes tends to be sticky and to attach itself to the kitchen paper, so lift the potatoes off the paper as soon as they are cooked.

MASHED POTATO

1 × 225 g (8 oz) jacket potato
Butter
Salt
Pepper
Milk

Scrub the potato, prick deeply with a fork, then place on a piece of kitchen paper in the microwave oven.

Cook, uncovered, on Full Power for 3 minutes; turn the potato over and continue cooking until it is soft.

Cut the potato in half, scoop out the pulp and with a fork mash with butter, salt and pepper, adding milk to taste.

MUSHROOMS À LA GRECQUE

Although mushrooms à la Grecque are really a starter, they are very good when reheated and served as an accompanying vegetable. Clean white button mushrooms are available at most greengrocers and I particularly like the boxed kind in the supermarket. A wipe with a piece of crumpled kitchen paper is all that is necessary to clean them.

About 100 g (4 oz) button mushrooms
5 tablespoons water
1 teaspoon olive oil
Salt
1 spring onion, trimmed and chopped
1 level teaspoon freshly chopped parsley
Pinch celery seeds
Pinch fennel seeds
Pinch dried thyme
1 teaspoon fresh lemon juice
1 tablespoon white wine
Freshly ground black pepper

1 litre (1¾ pint) bowl

Cut the mushrooms into quarters and mix with all the other ingredients in a 1 litre (1¾ pint) bowl. Cook, without covering, on Full Power for 2½ minutes or until the liquid begins to boil, then cook for a further 2 minutes.

Transfer the mushrooms to a serving dish and continue cooking the liquid, uncovered, on Full Power for about 5 minutes until only 2 tablespoons of liquid remain. Pour this over the mushrooms and leave until cold.

OVEN CHIPS

A handful of frozen chipped potatoes

Browning dish

Put the oven chips on a suitable plate and cook, without covering, on Full Power for about 1 minute until the chill is taken off.

Heat a browning dish to the maximum recommended by the manufacturer, then spread the chips over the surface in a single layer and cook, without covering, on Full Power for 30 seconds. Immediately toss the chips so that the upper surfaces are now against the browning dish and cook, without covering, for a further 30 seconds. The quicker you can toss the chips, the more crisp they will be.

Serve at once but be careful not to put the hot browning dish on a laminated work surface.

Note: The quantity you can cook at any one time depends upon the size of the browning dish that you are using; however you can cook a second batch while you are eating the first. To do this you will only need to reheat the unwashed browning dish for about 2 minutes because there will be quite a lot of residual heat left in the dish.

PASTA

Dried pasta keeps for ages so that it won't matter whether you buy a small or a large packet. Just take out the amount required, then seal the packet and put it away again in the larder.

Freshly made pasta, whether home-made or shop-bought, is much quicker to cook. If you have to buy a minimum quantity, store the surplus in the freezer – *not* in the refrigerator because it will soon start to go bad, the first sign of which is black speckling.

50 g (2 oz) is an average one-portion snack size and 75–100 g (3–4 oz) a single main-course size.

There is no saving of time when pasta is cooked by microwave but it does reduce the washing up and the possibility of sticking and burning. Overspill can be mopped up effortlessly.

Pasta needs plenty of water and swells during cooking so use a large bowl or casserole. Small pasta shapes will undoubtedly cook faster than, say, cannelloni or lasagne leaves. Frozen or left-over pasta can be reheated on Full Power – sprinkle with 2 tablespoons of water and cover during reheating, stirring occasionally. Cook for a minimum time and leave a standing time before draining.

Dried Pasta:

First put on the kettle to boil the water, and choose a suitable 1.95 litre (3½ pint) bowl or casserole. Put a teaspoon of oil and ½–1 teaspoon salt in the bowl.

Place small pasta shapes into the bowl *before* adding 600 ml (1 pint) boiling water, but if using spaghetti lower this in *after* putting the same amount of boiling water in the bowl.

Place the bowl in the microwave and cook, without covering, on Full Power for 1 minute. Stir to mix in any protruding spaghetti strands.

Cook for a further 5–6 minutes, stirring once during this period. Test to see whether the pasta is nearly cooked; cover the bowl tightly and leave to stand for 5 minutes, then test again. If necessary, cover and leave for a few more minutes.

Drain through a collander but do not shake every last drop of water away as the hot pasta will absorb the remainder.

If serving with a sauce, either cook the pasta last or cook it before making the sauce and reheat just before mixing in the sauce.

Fresh Pasta:

As for dried pasta, but reduce the cooking time to 2 minutes.

Stuffed Fresh Pasta:
As for dried pasta, but increase the cooking time by 3 to 4 minutes.

Wholemeal Pasta:
This takes about the same time as the ordinary white or green varieties.

PLAIN COOKED CABBAGE

Cabbage takes longer to cook than you think and contrary to expectation it cooks quicker in more rather than less water. Before cooking, remove the thick part of the stalk which you can either discard or chop up and use in salads (the stalk and tough stems of the cabbage can represent about one-eighth of the total weight).

225 g (8 oz) washed and trimmed cabbage
6–8 tablespoons water
Salt

1.1 litre (2 pint) casserole

Shred the cabbage finely. Put the water in a 1.1 litre (2 pint) casserole, stir in the salt to taste, then add the cabbage. Cover with the lid and cook on Full Power for 6 minutes. Stir, then test to see if the cabbage is done. If it is not ready, replace the lid and cook for a further 3–4 minutes. Drain and serve hot.

Note: Although cabbage is best served freshly cooked, to avoid any vitamin loss, nevertheless it can be reheated. Either reheat in the covered dish, adding one tablespoon cold water and allowing 2–3 minutes on Full Power, or reheat on your dinner plate together with the other ingredients of your meal.

POTATO SALAD

1 cooked but slightly firm jacket potato, weighing about
   200 g (7 oz)
2 level tablespoons mayonnaise
1 level teaspoon dried chopped chives

Skin the potato and cut into cubes. Put into a bowl and
mix in the mayonnaise and chives.

POTATO SKINS

If you are not in the habit of eating the skins of jacket
potatoes or have used the flesh for mashing, keep the
skins and make them into a crispy snack. Dunk the
crisped skins into a dip made of soured cream, lemon
juice and chives, seasoned with salt and freshly ground
black pepper.

Cooked skins from 2 or 3 jacket potatoes
25 g (1 oz) butter

Cut the cooked skins in half. Put the butter into a shallow
dish and heat on Full Power for 30–60 seconds until
melted.

Add the potato skins, turning them over so that they
are fully coated with the butter, and cook on Full Power
for 4–7 minutes until the skins are crispy.

Drain the skins on kitchen paper and discard the melted
butter.

RATATOUILLE

No matter how I tried to cut down the quantity in this
recipe I still found that it was too much for one person.
However, since it can be reheated, or indeed frozen to be

thawed and reheated, and is also delicious cold as a salad accompaniment, it doesn't matter if you err on the generous side.

1 tablespoon vegetable oil
½ clove garlic, peeled and crushed
½ small green pepper, seeded and finely sliced
½ small red pepper, seeded and finely sliced
2 courgettes, topped, tailed and sliced fairly thinly
2 tomatoes, quartered
¼ level teaspoon dried basil
Salt
Freshly ground black pepper

1.25 litre (2¼ pint) casserole

In a 1.25 litre (2¼ pint) casserole, combine the oil, garlic, green and red peppers. Cover with the lid and cook on Full Power for 3 minutes.

Stir in the courgettes and tomatoes, replace the lid and cook for a further 4 minutes on Full Power.

Remove the casserole lid, stir in the basil and season to taste with salt and pepper. Cook, without covering, on Full Power for a further 3–5 minutes or until the vegetables are tender.

Note: When other ingredients are being cooked to go with the ratatouille, it is best to cook the ratatouille first and keep it covered. It can easily be reheated at the last moment for 1–2 minutes.

RECONSTITUTING INSTANT POTATO POWDER

The amount of water required will depend upon which brand of dried potato you use. The quantities may have to be adjusted in the light of your own experience but as a rule, 1 level tablespoon potato powder will absorb approximately 3 tablespoons water.

Small Portion
2 level tablespoons instant potato powder
6 tablespoons water
Knob of butter
White pepper
Salt

0.55 litre (1 pint) bowl

Large Portion
4 level tablespoons instant potato powder
12 tablespoons water
Knob of butter
White pepper
Salt

0.55 litre (1 pint) bowl

Put the potato powder into an 0.55 litre (1 pint) bowl, pour the water over and add the knob of butter. Without covering, cook on Full Power for about 1 minute for the small portion and 2 minutes for the larger portion, stirring vigorously with a fork when the mixture bubbles and thickens. Season lightly with pepper, adding salt only after tasting.

Should the mixture be too thick, whisk in a little more hot water; if too thin, add a little extra potato powder which, provided it is whisked in quickly, will be absorbed without causing lumpiness or graining.

RICE

Long-grain rice cooks very well in the microwave oven but the amount of water that you need depends upon the rice that you buy as some absorb more liquid than others. I find the easy-cook rice is a success every time but this does not mean that ordinary patna and basmati are not just as good.

I usually cook a large quantity at one time, perhaps even up to 450 g (1 lb), using a 3.8 litre (5 pint) bowl. I then freeze the cooked rice in individual portions. To thaw and reheat, simply tip the rice on to a plate and heat on Full Power for 1–3 minutes. Cold cooked rice will keep in the refrigerator for a day or two, after which it tends to become sour. To reheat, sprinkle 1–2 teaspoons water over the rice and heat on Full Power, covered or uncovered, for 1–1½ minutes, stirring once during reheating.

Rice, when cooked, swells to three times its dry weight, so the more rice you cook, the more water is required. Rice is very good natured in its cooking and will not object if you start with cold water, in which case cooking will take a little longer; if you start with boiling water, there will be a slightly shorter cooking time. If you are cooking by the traditionla method, it is best not to cover the bowl because of the strong risk of boiling over. When using the measured quantity (modern) method, whether you cover the bowl or not makes little difference; you will need slightly more water than is recommended on the packet instructions.

Brown rice, which is more nutritious and wholesome than refined white rice, should be cooked in a measured amount of water so that all the goodness is retained. This rice takes considerably longer to cook than the white variety.

Rice pudding made with milk is more successful if cooked mainly on the Defrost (30 per cent) setting; pudding rice can also be cooked in water, on Full Power, subsequently adding condensed or evaporated milk.

BOILED RICE (TRADITIONAL METHOD)

Long-grain rice
Water
Salt

Large bowl

Put the rice a few tablespoons at a time into a strainer and wash under hot or cold running water, then tip the rice into a large bowl.

Boil an entire kettleful of water. Pour on to the rice and add ½–1 teaspoon salt. Stir thoroughly then cook, without covering, on Full Power for 10–15 minutes or until a grain of the rice will break easily when pressed with the side of a fork.

Put a colander in the sink and pour the rice into it allowing the starchy liquid to drain away. Run the cold tap through the rice until all the grains feel cool. Prop up the colander on the draining board or over the bowl that you have used for cooking and allow every last drop of water to drain through.

Reheat as much as is required (which takes 1–2 minutes) then refrigerate or freeze the remainder.

BOILED RICE (MODERN METHOD)

50 g (2 oz) easy-cook long-grain rice
150 ml (¼ pint) hot water
¼–½ teaspoon salt

1.25 litre (2¼ pint) casserole

Put the rice in a 1.25 litre (2¼ pint) casserole, add the water and salt and stir once. Cover with the lid and cook on Full Power for about 8 minutes, then test the rice to see if it is nearly cooked. If this is so stir quickly, replace the lid and set aside for 5 minutes before serving. If after this initial cooking time the rice is not quite cooked but all the liquid has been absorbed, add 2–3 tablespoons hot water, replace the lid and continue cooking on Full Power for a further 2–3 minutes.

Should cooked rice be too wet to serve, drain through a colander.

SCALLOPED POTATOES GRATINÉE

Cook the potatoes in a dish that is flameproof so that it will not shatter while under the grill. An oval pie dish has worked satisfactorily for me and should be all right provided that it is not placed too close to the element – I advise a distance of 4 cm (3 in).

225 g (8 oz) medium-sized potatoes
Salt
Freshly ground black pepper
15 g (½ oz) butter or margarine
1 small onion, peeled and finely chopped
25 g (1 oz) grated Cheddar cheese

0.4 litre (¾ pint) pie dish

Peel and thinly slice the potatoes and season with salt and pepper. Put the butter in a large bowl and cook, without covering, on Full Power for 30 seconds or until melted.

Stir in the onion and cook, without covering, on Full Power for 2 minutes to just soften the onion. Add half the cheese and then the potato slices, turning so that they are coated on both sides with the mixture.

Spread the potatoes in an 0.4 litre (¾ pint) oval pie dish and smooth the top. Cover the top of the dish loosely with cling film and cook on Full Power for 5 minutes.

Test for 'doneness' by pressing through the cling film against the potatoes with the back of a fork.

Carefully remove the cling film, sprinkle the potatoes with the remaining cheese, then brown under the grill.

SPINACH

Fresh Spinach:

The best way to cook spinach is in a roasting bag because more steam heat is created. An average portion is 225 g (8 oz) bought weight which, of course, is reduced almost by half when the stems have been removed. After washing in plenty of cold water and without undue draining, put the leaves in a roasting bag. Seal loosely with an elastic band. (Remember you must never use metal tags in the microwave, even when covered in paper or plastic.) Pull the top of the roasting bag apart so that there is a gap through the elastic band, then cook on Full Power for about 4 minutes. The leaves will pack down in the bag and you should be able to drain off the water by holding the bag upside-down (possibly using oven gloves to combat the heat) and the liquid should drain out through the hole. Remove the elastic band, take the spinach out of the bag and chop or cut up with kitchen scissors.

Frozen Spinach:

Put the block of spinach, whether chopped or leaf, in a suitable dish (not on a plate because frozen spinach creates quite a lot of water, more than a plate could accommodate). Cook, without covering, on Full Power for 3–4 minutes, breaking up the block two or three times during cooking, pushing the still-frozen parts towards the outside of the dish. As soon as the spinach is thawed but still cold, cover with a lid or vented cling film and continue cooking on Full Power for a minute or two longer or until the spinach is hot. Add salt after cooking.

SUPER SWEDES

Peeling swedes is laborious and hazardous. A very sharp knife and chopping board are essential. Prepare and cook this way instead.

1 small whole swede
Water
Butter
Salt
Pepper

Rinse the swede to remove any adhering mud and place in a roasting bag. Add 1–1½ cups water.

Seal the roasting bag loosely with a large elastic band and place upright on the oven base or turntable. Cook on Full Power for 7–8 minutes.

Leave to stand for 5 minutes, then carefully open the bag and take out the swede. Put the swede on a board and using a sharp knife and fork peel carefully. Cut up, then chop or purée the flesh, adding the butter and seasoning to taste. Put into a covered serving dish and reheat on Full Power for 30 seconds.

In the unlikely event of the swede remaining under-cooked, extend the reheating time and stir frequently.

TAGLIATELLE NESTS

Tagliatelle nests are the quickest cooking of the dried pastas. Although called 'nests' the pasta strips separate during cooking. The cooked pasta reheats well when mixed with a sauce.

300 ml (½ pint) water
Salt
½ teaspoon vegetable oil

2–3 nests of tagliatelle
Knob of butter

0.85 litre (1½ pint) bowl

Put the water, salt and oil into an 0.85 litre (1½ pint) bowl and cook, without covering, on Full Power for 2 minutes or until the water boils. Quickly put in the tagliatelle nests and make sure that they are completely immersed. Cover very loosely with cling film, but do not vent. Cook on Full Power for 3 minutes, then allow a standing time of 1 minute.

Pierce the cling film with a sharp knife before carefully uncovering. Drain away any surplus liquid and stir in the butter.

VEGETABLE MARROW

Whatever you do with marrow, unless it is stuffed or sauced it has very little flavour; nevertheless the colour is good and the vegetable goes with most meat dishes. It is easy to prepare and fairly quick to cook. The smallest size that you are likely to be able to obtain is 675 g (1½ lb) but by the time you have peeled and seeded the vegetable and because it contains so much water, you will probably finish up with 225–350 g (½–¾ lb) of vegetable – a reasonable serving. If you like to eat raw vegetables as salad ingredients, then marrow is pleasant when served with well-seasoned yogurt to which has been added a squeeze of fresh lemon juice.

225 g (8 oz) vegetable marrow
Salt
Freshly ground black pepper

1.25 litre (2¼ pint) casserole

Remove the peel, cut the marrow in half lengthwise and scoop out the seeds. Cut the flesh into 1 cm (½ in) slices, then cut these in half to resemble pineapple chunks.

Put the marrow pieces into a 1.25 litre (2¼ pint) casserole, cover with the lid and cook for 5–7 minutes. Allow a standing time of 3 minutes, then remove the lid, drain away the juices and season the marrow generously with salt and pepper.

Cakes, Puddings and Desserts

Unless you are treating yourself to a special dinner you will be looking for a dessert that can be served either cold or reheated.

Old-fashioned sponge puddings not only cook well, but reheat well too. You can easily cook small ones in the microwave oven, because the choice of containers is so much greater. Cook the pudding in a small bowl, breakfast cup, mug or Pyrex jug. No oven gloves are needed for turning out the pudding, and if the vessel has a handle this will not get hot.

A three-portion cake made in a jug is quick and easy and you won't have left-over portions to get stale. Always use a bowl, jug or cake shape of a size that will allow for the mixture rising during the cooking process. Cake mixtures cooked in a microwave oven rise rapidly and if the container is not big enough, there can be an overspill before the batters become set and cooked. My students often find it strange to see me demonstrating with such large bowls, when the finished item is so small. This is just another microwave idiosyncrasy. Only half-fill basins or cake shapes with raw batter, which latter should be a little wetter than if being cooked in a conventional oven. Place small containers in the centre of the microwave oven.

Remember that syrups or jams spooned into the base of the container will become too hot for some plastic shapes. I am not a great 'plastic fan', but I do recommend some of the cake shapes and I have included these in my list on page 28. Plastic containers do not usually need greasing, and a light film of butter, smeared over the container with a butter paper or a small snippet of kitchen paper, is quite sufficient for greasing all other types. You can buy packets or round or square ready-cut non-stick liners, which ensure that none of the cooked mixture is left stuck in the dish.

Individual small cakes are convenient and for these you can either use ramekin dishes (also available in plastic) or paper cases.

Chocolate, ginger and fruit cakes are all attractively brown-looking and so do not need any disguise. Pale cakes, such as Madeira, do not brown in the microwave and look better iced or decorated. Icings are soon prepared and can be made up previously if preferred.

Most plain cakes and sponge puddings should be cooked on Full Power until they appear almost dry on top and start to come away from the sides of the dish. Follow this cooking period, unless otherwise stated, with a 5–10 minute standing time, during which the underneath catches up. This is very important. After turning out, should the top (which was the bottom!) seem moist, place on a suitable plate, moist side uppermost, and cook without covering for a further minute.

Don't ignore packet cake and puddings mixes – the cakes are especially nice. Follow the instructions on the packet but cook by microwave in a suitably sized dish until the 'doneness' signs are visible.

All fruit desserts can be cooked by microwave and do not require a standing time.

Use the microwave to dissolve gelatine; for cooking meringue-topped puddings when the meringue will have a mallow-like texture; and for crumbles, subsequently browning under the grill if desired.

Large frozen cakes can be partially thawed in the microwave on the 10 per cent setting (or no 1) and will take about 6–8 minutes; small individual cakes will take 2–3 minutes for two. Cream cakes and iced cakes must be thawed at room temperature as the microwaves quickly melt fresh cream and sugary icings. 20–30 seconds on Full Power is usually sufficient to heat a single portion of cold pudding. Thaw and reheat a single portion on Full Power for about 1–2 minutes; a large pudding on the Defrost (30 per cent) setting for about 5 minutes.

THE RECIPES

QUICK COOKING

Baked Apple
Canterbury Bread Pudding
Carruthers Pudding
Cherry Yogurt Pudding
Floating Islands

Individual Ginger Cakes
Peach Upside-down Pudding
Pineapple Flambé
Zabaglione

MODERATELY QUICK COOKING

Bread and Butter Pudding
Superior Chocolate Cake
Torta Farcita All'Arancia

SLOW COOKING

Brandied Chocolate Mousse
Caramel Oranges
Christmas Pudding
Crème Brulée
Crème Caramel

Lemon Soufflé
Lime Mousse
Rice Pudding
Stewed Dried Fruit

BAKED APPLE

The baked apple is one of the most difficult desserts to cook by microwave but it is also one of the quickest. The stumbling block is that even when the skin is well scored and a sliver removed from each end of the apple, the pulp tends to rise with volcanic energy. The apple completely collapses and the skin remains tough. A batch of four apples is much more likely to be successful than a single fruit. You *can* bake one apple on Full Power but I can promise greater success if the Defrost (30 per cent) setting is used. In the event of a collapse either call it smashed apple or remove the skin and use the pulp as stewed apple – delicious mixed with a tablespoon of cream.

1 × 200–225 g (7–8 oz) cooking apple
1 level tablespoon soft brown sugar
1 tablespoon water, cider or wine
1 level tablespoon sultanas, raisins or mixed dried fruit

Cereal bowl

Rinse, dry and core the apple and make a cut around the 'waist' with a stainless steel knife.

Stir the sugar and water together in a suitable cereal bowl. Stand the apple in the centre of the bowl, open end up, and fill the cavity with dried fruit.

Cook, without covering, on Defrost (30 per cent) for 2½–3 minutes until the apple has partly changed colour. Turn the apple over and cook, without covering, on Defrost (30 per cent) for a further 2–2½ minutes – both top and bottom of the apple will have changed colour, leaving a narrow 'waistband' of green. Cover the bowl completely and leave to stand for 5 minutes until the colour equalizes and the fruit is cooked.

CANTERBURY BREAD PUDDING

A good old-fashioned solid pudding which although best eaten hot is also acceptable cold. Serve plain or with cream or custard.

2–3 level tablespoons marmalade
2 slices white bread
2 level tablespoons dark soft brown sugar
1 level tablespoon soft margarine
2 level tablespoons self-raising flour
2 teaspoons milk
¼ teaspoon vinegar

0.3 litre (½ pint) bowl, cereal bowl or cup

Grease an 0.3 litre (½ pint) bowl or cup and spread the sides and base with the marmalade.

Put the bread in a dish and cover with cold water, then when the bread has soaked up as much moisture as it will take, squeeze it out as dry as possible. This is a rather messy task but you can do it with a fork.

Beat together the sugar and margarine, then add the flour. When this is well mixed in, add the bread, milk and vinegar. Beat thoroughly and spoon into the marmaladed bowl, making sure that the mixture reaches only two-thirds up.

Cover with a circle of greaseproof or non-stick paper that will fit neatly inside the rim and cook on Defrost (30 per cent) for 6–8 minutes, depending on how solid you wish the pudding to be.

When turned out on to a serving plate, the pudding will have a coating of marmalade.

CARRUTHERS PUDDING

The 'taster's' comment was that the appearance is not too
good but it tastes great. *I* thought it looked good too.
When browned under the grill, the top has a nice golden
glow and the natural pink colour of the raspberries is
most appetizing. The pudding is equally good when served
cold.

    25 g (1 oz) butter
    4 level tablespoons self-raising flour
    Salt
    Pinch bicarbonate of soda
    2 level tablespoons porridge oats
    2–3 level tablespoons demerara sugar
    5 tablespoons milk
    225 g (½ lb) raspberries, or a mixture of raspberries
        and sliced cooking apples

    0.4 litre (¾ pint) flameproof pie dish, greased

Rub the butter into the flour until of a crumble-like
consistency, then stir in the salt, bicarbonate of soda,
porridge oats and sugar. Add the milk and mix thoroughly
(the consistency will be similar to a heavy batter). Stir in
the fruit.

Well grease an 0.4 litre (¾ pint) flameproof pie dish.
Pour the mixture into the prepared dish and cook, without
covering, on Full Power for 5 minutes. Test for 'doneness', and if the pudding is still very soft in the middle
cook for an additional minute.

Brown the pudding under the grill and serve as it is or
with fresh whipped cream.

CHERRY YOGURT PUDDING

I devised this recipe to use up surplus egg whites and although the portion is rather large for one, it does reheat well taking only ½–1 minute on Full Power.

2 tablespoons egg white
3 level tablespoons self-raising flour
2 level tablespoons caster sugar
2 level tablespoons soft margarine
150 ml (¼ pint) low-fat black cherry yogurt

0.4 litre (¾ pint) pie dish, greased

Well grease an 0.4 litre (¾ pint) pie dish and set aside. Whisk the egg white until fairly stiff (when a peak of the mixture just curves over when lifted on the whisk).

In another bowl but using the same beaters, whisk the flour, sugar and margarine together (the mixture will resemble soft crumbs). Whisk in 2 level tablespoons of the yogurt, then fold the egg white into the mixture with a metal tablespoon.

Pour into the prepared pie dish and cook, without covering, on Full Power for 3 minutes or until the top of the pudding is just set.

Pour over the remaining yogurt and cook, without covering, on Full Power for 30 seconds.

Serve warm.

FLOATING ISLANDS

This is the smallest quantity that can be cooked as it is impossible to split one egg yolk and one egg white. The dessert is delicious whether eaten hot or cold, so any surplus can be finished up next day. Should you have a dinner guest, serve the floating islands on a slice of jam

Swiss roll, reheating briefly on the Defrost (30 per cent)
setting.

2 level tablespoons caster sugar
1 level teaspoon cornflour
Pinch salt
150 ml (¼ pint) milk
¼ teaspoon vanilla essence
1 small egg, separated
¼ teaspooon fresh lemon juice
Dairy Flake bar

Shallow 15 cm (6 in) dish
1 litre (1¾ pint) bowl

Mix 1 tablespoon of the sugar with the cornflour, salt,
milk, vanilla essence and egg yolk in a 1 litre (1¾ pint)
bowl. Cook, without covering, on Full Power for 1
minute. Beat thoroughly with a wire whisk, then continue
cooking for a further 1½–2 minutes, whisking every 30
seconds, until the custard thickens slightly.

Pour the custard into a 15 cm (6 in) shallow dish and
set aside while making the meringue.

Using grease-free beaters, whisk the egg white until
stiff. Whisk in the remaining sugar a teaspoonful at a
time then fold in the lemon juice.

Using a tablespoon, scoop out four oval shapes of the
meringue and place them round the edge of the custard.
Reduce the setting and cook, without covering, on
Defrost (30 per cent) for 4 minutes or until the meringue
is just set and mallow-like

Leave to cool, then sprinkle with the crushed Dairy
Flake bar.

INDIVIDUAL GINGER CAKES

Using double-thickness individual cake cases retains a nice round shape. The recipe makes 12 and the cakes will keep for a few days in an airtight container. Have the cakes for tea, with your nightcap, in your lunch box or simply when you feel like a snack. The batter can be cooked in an ungreased 1 litre (1½ pint) bowl for serving as a hot pudding which takes about 2½–3 minutes to cook.

1 tablespoon clear honey
1 tablespoon black treacle or molasses
2 tablespoons salad oil
1 tablespoon milk
25 g (1 oz) soft dark brown sugar
50 g (2 oz) granary flour
⅛ level teaspoon bicarbonate of soda
Pinch salt
1–1½ level teaspoons ground ginger
1 small egg (size 5)

1 microwave-suitable mixing bowl
24 individual paper cake cases

Put one paper case inside another so that you have 12 double-thickness cases.

Put the honey, treacle or molasses, oil, milk and sugar into a microwave-suitable mixing bowl and stir with a wire whisk. Cook, without covering, on Full Power for 1 minute, stirring once during that period. Stir until the sugar has dissolved.

Sift in the flour, bicarbonate of soda, salt and ground ginger. Reserve the coarse wheaty bits left in the sieve.

Stir in the egg and mix thoroughly into the batter.

Divide the mixture between the cake cases putting about 1 level tablespoon in each. If your oven is fitted with a turntable, remove this from the cavity and arrange six of the filled cases in a circle on the turntable. Carefully replace it in the microwave and cook, without covering, on Full Power for 45–60 seconds, until the cakes have risen and are only just dry on top. They must still be slightly moist at the edges. Remove the cakes and the turntable, then arrange and similarly cook the second batch. Sprinkle the hot cakes with the reserved wheaty bits. (In an oven without a turntable, carefully transfer the filled cases to the oven with the aid of a fish slice. If you do it by hand the sides may be accidentally squeezed, causing the mixture to spill out.)

PEACH UPSIDE-DOWN PUDDING

With this recipe you can ring the changes by using apricots, mandarin oranges or pineapple instead of peaches, but do be sure to buy canned fruit in fresh juice and not the in-syrup kind.

Although best eaten hot, the pudding is acceptable when served cold. It can also be reheated the next day. Should you intend to do this, keep the left-over fruit juice in a cup or bowl in the refrigerator, then pour the juice over the pudding before reheating. There will be no need to reverse the pudding – it is perfectly satisfactory to pour the juice directly over the fruit.

2 level tablespoons soft dark brown sugar
1 level tablespoon softened butter or soft margarine
1 × 213 g (7½ oz) can peach slices in fruit juice
1 egg
1 heaped tablespoon self-raising flour
2 level tablespoons caster sugar
1 tablespoon salad oil (not olive)

0.4 litre (¾ pint) pie dish

Put the sugar and butter or margarine into an 0.4 litre (¾ pint) pie dish and cook, without covering, on Full Power for 30 seconds. Stir until blended, making sure that the entire base of the dish is coated with the mixture. Drain the fruit, reserving the juice, and arrange the peach slices decoratively on top of the sugar mixture.

Break the egg into a jug, beat lightly, then mix in the flour, sugar and oil to form a soft batter. Pour this over the fruit and cook, without covering, on Full Power for about 3 minutes or until the mixture is just dry on top. Leave to stand for 2 minutes, then pour about half of the fruit juice evenly over the top. This should soak in quickly. Turn the pudding out on to a hot serving dish.

PINEAPPLE FLAMBÉ

It is very important to use a flameproof dish for any food that is to be flambéed.

1 level teaspoon butter
1 level teaspoon flaked almonds
1 slice fresh pineapple, trimmed
1 level tablespoon icing sugar, sieved
1 tablespoon Kirsch

Suitable flameproof dish

Put the butter and almonds into a suitable flameproof dish and cook, without covering, on Full Power for 2 minutes, stirring once during cooking.

Add the pineapple and then turn it over so that both sides of the fruit are coated with the butter.

Sift over the icing sugar, using a clean tea strainer, then cook, without covering, on Full Power for 30 seconds.

Turn the pineapple over once more and cook, without

covering, for a further 30 seconds. Remove the dish from the microwave oven.

Pour the Kirsch into a suitable egg cup or glass and cook, without covering, on Full Power for 10 seconds which should be just sufficient to warm the Kirsch. Immediately pour the Kirsch over the pineapple and ignite.

Preferably leave the flames to die down on their own but if you are nervous about the strength of the serving dish, then blow them out.

ZABAGLIONE

This rich dessert is best served warm, although it is equally delicious cold. However, when cold the mixture tends to sink and so would look better with a rosette of whipped cream on top. Ideally zagablione should be served in a stemmed glass accompanied by sponge finger biscuits or ice cream wafers. If the wine is heated in a glass in the microwave be sure not to use one of your best glasses and most certainly not if they are crystal, since this has a metal content. Should you possess only expensive crystal glasses, it is best to heat the wine in a cup or suitable bowl.

The recipe can be doubled, allowing an extra few seconds at each cooking stage.

    1 whole egg
    1 egg yolk
    2 level tablespoons caster sugar
    3 tablespoons sherry or Madeira

    1 litre (1¾ pint) bowl

Beat the whole egg and the egg yolk together, then strain into a 1 litre (1¾ pint) bowl. Add the sugar and beat with an electric whisk until the mixture is thick. It should be possible to scoop out a spoonful without the mixture falling from the bowl of the spoon.

Put the sherry or Madeira in an ordinary wine glass or cup and cook, uncovered, on Full Power for 45 seconds or until the wine begins to bubble. Immediately pour it on to the egg mixture and beat vigorously.

Replace the bowl in the microwave oven and cook, without covering, for 1 minute, whisking every 15 seconds, until the dessert is thick but creamy. Do not overcook or curdling will occur; if this should happen, sometimes it is possible to beat out a curdle provided you catch it in time.

Pour the zabaglione into the wine glass and serve warm or refrigerate until required.

BREAD AND BUTTER PUDDING

If you prefer a softer pudding you could use buttered bread instead of toast, but the colour will be pale and, although really delicious to eat, would look better if lightly browned under the grill. Sometimes I use this method if custardy mixtures have not quite set in the middle, because the heat of the grill is sufficient to just complete the cooking, whereas over-microwaving would spoil it.

It does not matter which dried fruits you use – chopped apricots, peaches or pears make an interesting change.

2 slices toast
Butter
50 g (2 oz) mixed dried fruit or a selection of currants,
    raisins and sultanas
150 ml (¼ pint) milk
1 egg

2 level tablespoons demerara sugar
¼ level teaspoon cinnamon

0.4 litre (¾ pint) pie dish

Remove the crusts and butter the toast on one side, then cut each slice into four triangles.

Arrange four of the toast triangles butter-side down against the base of an 0.4 litre (¾ pint) pie dish, then sprinkle with half the dried fruit. Cover with the remaining toast triangles, then sprinkle with the remaining dried fruit.

Beat together in a bowl the milk, egg, sugar and cinnamon and pour evenly into the dish.

Cover the dish with vented cling film and cook on Defrost (30 per cent) for 8–10 minutes or until the custard is set around the edges. Do not be tempted to overcook or the custard will separate.

SUPERIOR CHOCOLATE CAKE

A tried and trusted recipe that is surprisingly easy to make. I used one of the new 1 litre (1¾ pints) Pyrex measuring jugs which has a diameter of 12.5 cm (5 in) at the top, but any suitable round container having straight sides, such as a small undecorated soufflé dish or plastic cake shape, will do. The narrower diameter produces a nice tall cake. If using a wider dish (for example 15 cm (6 in) wide), the cake will be rather flat, will be quicker to cook and is best halved vertically.

Either grease the sides and line the base of your chosen container with a disc of non-stick paper or loosely line with crumpled cling film. When lining with cling film, make sure that there are plenty of wrinkles in the plastic to allow for shrinkage and also ensure that you have an overhang of cling film which will make it cleaner and simpler when the cake is turned out.

50 g (2 oz) margarine or butter
50 g (2 oz) golden syrup
1 egg, beaten
40 g (1½ oz) self-raising flour
1 level teaspoon baking powder
2 level tablespoons cocoa powder

For the filling:
2–3 level tablespoons apricot jam

For the icing:
25 g (1 oz) butter
1 tablespoon milk
10 level tablespoons (approx.) icing sugar
2 level tablespoons cocoa powder

12½ cm (5 in) diameter round deep dish
1 litre (1¾ pint) bowl

First prepare and line a 12.5 cm (5 in) diameter round deep dish. Put the margarine or butter and syrup into a 1 litre (1¾ pint) bowl and heat, without covering, on Full Power for 1 minute or until melted.

Sift the flour, baking powder and cocoa powder over the mixture, stir, then add the egg and beat thoroughly for 1 minute.

Pour the cake batter into the prepared dish and cook, without covering, on Full Power for 1½–2 minutes or until the cake is just set on top. If the cake dish has been lined with cling film, it should be turned out immediately; if the dish has been greased and lined, leave the cake to stand for 5 minutes before turning out. Leave to cool.

Cut the cake in half and sandwich with the jam. Place on a cooling wire over a tray.

To make the icing, first put the butter and milk in a bowl or jug and cook, without covering, on Full Power for 30 seconds or until the butter has melted. Sift in the icing sugar and cocoa powder and beat until smooth. Pour the icing over the top of the cake. With care, tip the wire rack from side to side so that the icing falls evenly over the sides of the cake. If necessary, warm a table knife with hot water and use to spread the icing more evenly. Leave until set before transferring the cake to a dish or container.

Sufficient for 4 servings

TORTA FARCITA ALL'ARANCIA

A loaf-shaped cake with an unusual cooked orange filling, covered with soft orange icing and suitable for serving as a gâteau or dessert. It is not possible to bake a smaller version but it is so delicious that you will quickly eat it up. My cake was cooked in a Pyrex loaf dish measuring 19 × 10 × 5 cm (7½ × 4 × 2 in) and with a capacity of 750 ml (1¼ pints), but you can use a round shape if you prefer. Whichever shape of dish you decide to use you must make sure that the uncooked mixture does not more than one-third fill it, as microwave-cooked cakes rise considerably. Timings also vary to some extent. Cook only until the cake is just dry on top, as overcooking cannot be remedied. The colour of the outside of the cake is no indicator of 'doneness' as microwaved cakes do not colour very much. However, when you cut a slice, you will see that the cake has a nice golden glow inside.

1 small orange
100 g (4 oz) butter or margarine
100 g (4 oz) golden syrup

2 eggs
100 g (4 oz) self-raising flour
½ level treaspoon baking powder
2–3 tablespoons apricot jam

For the icing
50 g (2 oz) butter
2 tablespoons orange juice, left over from the orange
225 g (8 oz) icing sugar

Small glass loaf dish or 15 cm (16 in) round cake dish
1.1 litre (2 pint) bowl.

Grease a small glass loaf dish (or a 15 cm (6 in) pound cake dish) and line the base with non-stick paper.

Finely grate the orange rind and set aside.

Put the butter and syrup in a 1.1 litre (2 pint) bowl and cook, without covering, on Full Power for 1½ minutes or until melted.

Beat the eggs and add to the mixture beating well.

Sift the flour and baking powder on to the mixture and beat thoroughly for 1 minute. (It should be of a heavy batter consistency.) Stir in the grated orange zest.

Pour the batter into the prepared dish and cook, without covering, on Full Power for 3 minutes or until the cake is just dry on top. Leave to cool in the dish for 5–10 minutes.

Turn out the cake on to a cooling wire and split in half horizontally.

To make the filling, using a sharp knife and sturdy board remove the peel and pith from the orange, then cut out the segments (discard the thin membrane which can be tough to eat). Do this over a bowl so that none of the juice is wasted. Reserve the juice.

Place the orange segments in a suitable bowl together with the apricot jam. Cook, without covering, on Full

Power for 1–1½ minutes or until the mixture thickens. Leave to cool.

Now prepare the icing. Put the butter and 2 tablespoons of the reserved orange juice into a bowl and cook, without covering, on Full Power for 1 minute or until the butter is nicely melted. (If you do not have the stated amount of orange juice, add a little water.) Sift in the icing sugar gradually and beat until the mixture is smooth.

To finish the cake, sandwich the two halves together with the orange/jam mixture. (It does not matter if the filling is runny and dribbles down the side of the cake.) Set the cake wider side uppermost on a wire grill over a tray to catch any icing that may drip off, then pour the surplus icing over the top and sides of the cake. Use a hot damp table knife to spread the icing evenly, leave for a few moments, then pull a fork through the icing to give a channelled effect.

Leave until cold, then serve as required. The icing should keep the cake moist inside, but unless the orange is cooked sufficiently in the apricot jam, the cake will keep for only a few days.

BRANDIED CHOCOLATE MOUSSE

The recipe is sufficient for just one goblet. Double the quantity if you wish and store the second portion in the refrigerator or freezer. You may need to allow an extra few seconds in the microwave for the chocolate to melt.

1 egg
25 g (1 oz) (about 4 squares) plain dessert chocolate
1 teaspoon cold water
Few drops brandy

0.55 litre (1 pint) bowl

Separate the egg, putting the white into a bowl that will be large enough to hold it when beaten.

Put the chocolate and water into an 0.55 litre (1 pint) bowl and cook on Full Power for about 1 minute or until the chocolate melts. Stir, then cook on Full Power for a further 20–30 seconds until the chocolate is sufficiently melted to mix easily with the water.

Lightly beat the egg yolk and stir into the chocolate mixture, then add the brandy. Leave until cool (this takes 10–15 minutes).

Using clean grease-free beaters, whisk the egg white until stiff, then fold into the chocolate mixture using a metal spoon.

Spoon the mousse into a stemmed goblet and chill before serving.

Note: For a dessert that is a little more 'upmarket', top with freshly whipped cream and grated chocolate and serve with fan-shaped wafers.

CARAMEL ORANGES

You must be on the spot when cooking syrups in the microwave as they colour rapidly. If not watched carefully syrups can burn, creating acrid brown fumes. An oven glove is vital as the jug will become very hot indeed and must be placed on a dry heatproof surface on removal from the oven. Making syrups, whether in a saucepan on the hob or by microwave, requires some practice but it is well worth persevering as they are so useful in dessert cookery. Remember that the cooking container must be resistant to very high temperatures – I prefer to use a Pyrex jug or bowl.

1–2 large oranges
Water
4 level tablespoons granulated sugar
1 teaspoon Curaçao or similar liqueur

Small cup or jug
0.55 litre (1 pint) jug or lipped bowl
Oven gloves

Peel and slice the oranges into rounds and spread them in a serving dish. Put about 2 tablespoons of water in a small cup or jug and heat, without covering, on Full Power for 1 minute or until boiling rapidly. Cover with a saucer to keep hot.

In an 0.55 litre (1 pint) jug or lipped bowl combine 2 tablespoons of water with the sugar and cook, without covering, on Full Power for 1 minute. Stir and continue cooking for a further 3–4 minutes or until the syrup is a light golden brown. Using oven gloves, quickly remove the jug of syrup from the microwave oven, place on a heatproof surface and immediately and carefully pour in the hot water that you have set aside. Do not stir but swirl the jug gently until the water is incorporated with the syrup.

Return the jug of syrup to the microwave and cook, without covering, on Full Power for 30 seconds. Pour in the liqueur and shake the jug gently, then pour the syrup over the oranges.

Chill for a few hours before serving.

CHRISTMAS PUDDING

There is enough for two generous portions in this recipe; it is not practical to reduce the quantities because any shorter cooking time would prevent the flavours from developing properly. Because the pudding is made with margarine rather than suet, it is far less greasy and so is perfectly acceptable served cold. Reheating is rapid; one portion will take only 30–60 seconds on Full Power. Take care not to over-reheat or you may burn your mouth!

150 g (5 oz) mixed dried fruit (e.g. sultanas, currants and raisins)
3 tablespoons sherry
2 tablespoons brandy
3 level tablespoons dark soft brown sugar
¼ level teaspoon ground mixed spice
25 g (1 oz) chopped mixed nuts
¼ green dessert apple, peeled, cored and finely chopped
Squeeze lemon juice
1 tablespoon black treacle
2 level tablespoons soft margarine
40 g (1½ oz) soft fresh brown breadcrumbs
1 egg, beaten
2 level tablespoons plain flour

0.55 litre (1 pint) basin

Grease an 0.55 litre (1 pint) basin and put a small circle of non-stick paper in the base.

In a suitable bowl, thoroughly mix 1 tablespoon of the brandy with the rest of the pudding ingredients then spoon the mixture into the prepared basin.

Cover loosely with cling film and cook in the centre of the microwave oven on Defrost (30 per cent) for 10 minutes. Remove the cling film and pour the remaining tablespoon of brandy over the warm pudding. Re-cover with cling film and leave until cold or overnight.

Turn out the pudding on to a microwave-proof serving dish and remove the paper disc. Reheat on Full Power for 2 minutes, then leave to stand for 3–4 minutes before serving.

Serve with fresh whipped cream or brandy butter.

CRÈME BRULÉE

This royal dessert used to be considered difficult to make but it is relatively simple with this recipe. There are three important points to observe:

(1) You must use a bowl similar to the one recommended because a narrow-diameter bowl reduces the chances of curdling.

(2) You must beat frequently and vigorously during cooking and cook only until the mixture is thick enough to retain an impression when a whisk is drawn through it. The start of a curdle can be identified by visible separation around the edges of the dish. Usually a quick and thorough beating will save the day.

(3) The syrup must be watched carefully and removed from the microwave when it is light brown – at a certain point during cooking the temperature rises rapidly, turning the syrup dark brown and then black. The syrup must be cooked in a glass measuring jug. Use rubber gloves to grasp the handle and to protect the other hand.

200 ml (7 fl oz) double cream
2 egg yolks, strained
⅔ level teaspoon cornflour
4 level teaspoons caster sugar

For the syrup:
2 tablespoons cold water
50 g (2 oz) granulated sugar

1 Pyrex measuring jug
1 litre (1¾ pint) bowl
2 individual ramekins

Using a 1 litre (1¾ pint) bowl, beat the cream, yolks, cornflour and caster sugar together thoroughly and cook, without covering, on Full Power for 2½–3 minutes, beating vigorously with a whisk at the end of each 30 seconds. As soon as the mixture is thick divide it between two ramekin dishes and, if necessary, smooth the tops with a knife.

Chill the desserts in the refrigerator until cold, or cover and freeze until required. Before preparing the topping, put the custards on a board or work surface near the microwave.

To make the syrup topping, stir the cold water and granulated sugar together in a Pyrex measuring jug and cook, without covering, on Full Power for 1 minute. Stir thoroughly, then cook for a further 2½ minutes or until the syrup is a light brown colour. Quickly pour a thin layer of the syrup over the chilled or frozen custards and leave until set and brittle. To test, pat the surface with a spoon.

Chilled brulée may be consumed immediately but if the topping has been put on to frozen custard, the ramekin should be left at room temperature for 30–60 minutes to thaw.

CRÈME CARAMEL

Cook this in a vessel which can withstand the very high temperature that hot syrups reach. When cooking the syrup, at first you will see bubbles appear around the sides of the jug. These bubbles will become larger and the syrup will boil up and slowly thicken. Suddenly, when you are least expecting it, the syrup will begin to darken and form the caramel, so it is inadvisable to leave the kitchen during the cooking.

After the pudding is turned out there will be a certain amount of residual caramel in the base of the jug or ramekin. Sometimes it is possible to refill with more custard, then cook in the same jug on top of this remaining caramel. (To facilitate cleaning, soak the jug in water for a few hours and you will find that the caramel will have dissolved.)

A well-cooked Crème Caramel is fabulous. The cooler it becomes, the more caramel sauce is produced, but this is not to say that you cannot eat it warm with equal enjoyment.

For the caramel:
2 level tablespoons caster sugar
2 tablespoons water

For the custard:
1 egg
1 level tablespoon caster sugar
7 tablespoons milk
¼ teaspoon vanilla essence

0.55 litre (1 pint) jug or bowl
Clean tea strainer

First make the caramel. Mix the sugar and water together in an 0.55 litre (1 pint) Pyrex jug or bowl. Stir thoroughly then cook, without covering, on Full Power until the syrup is dark brown but *not black*. Cooking continues after the microwave is switched off and overcooking will result in burning, producing acrid black fumes.

Using oven gloves, carefully stand the jug on a board or ultra-heatproof surface. Leave until cold, when the caramel will set hard as glass.

Now prepare the custard filling. Beat all the ingredients together in a bowl, then pour through a clean tea strainer on to the hardened caramel. Cover the jug or bowl with loose cling film and cook on 20 per cent power (or No 2) for 8–10 minutes or until the mixture is wobbly but nearly set. (If your microwave oven has two or three settings only, cook on Defrost (30 per cent) for 3 minutes.) Allow a standing time of 2 minutes, then cook for a further 2–3 minutes.

For the safest but slowest method of cooking, stand the covered jug in a suitable dish containing about 2.5 cm (1 in) hot water and microwave on Defrost (30 per cent) for 12–14 minutes. Leave until cold.

Note: Very often, although the custard is cooked around the edges, the middle may still be wobbly. As the Crème Caramel is best served cold, the length of standing time enables the middle to catch up. Overcooking is a big mistake although it is natural to think that further cooking will result in further setting. In fact it has the opposite effect – the whole mixture curdles and separates out.

LEMON SOUFFLÉ

There is enough for two servings here but the soufflés will keep for a few days in the refrigerator and for 1 or 2 weeks in the freezer if stored in a well-sealed box (thaw at room temperature before serving). During storage the mixture becomes a little more solid but this does not detract from its delicious lemon flavour.

  2 tablespoons fresh lemon juice (the bottled kind will
     not do)
  1 tablespoon water
  2–3 level tablespoons caster sugar
  1 level teaspoon powdered gelatine
  1 large egg, separated
  3 tablespoons double cream, whipped
  Grated chocolate, whipped cream or lemon jellies for
     decoration

  0.55 litre (1 pint) jug

Combine the lemon juice and water in an 0.55 litre (1 pint) jug and cook, without covering, on Full Power for 1 minute. Stir in the sugar until it has dissolved, then sprinkle the gelatine over the surface. Stir thoroughly and cook for 15 seconds. Stir, then leave to stand for 2 minutes. If after this time the gelatine has not completely dissolved, replace the jug in the microwave oven and heat on Full Power for a further 20–30 seconds. The mixture must not boil once the gelatine has been added.

Beat the egg yolk, then pour through a clean tea strainer into the gelatine mixture and beat thoroughly. Leave the jug in a cool place (but not the freezer) until the jelly is just beginning to set.

Beat in the cream, then using clean grease-free beaters, whip up the egg white until soft peaks form. Fold this into the mixture.

Pour the soufflé into one or two ramekins and chill before serving, decorated with grated chocolate, whipped cream or lemon jellies.

LIME MOUSSE

This flexible recipe allows you to use soft tub or an individual vanilla ice cream. Lemon, orange or raspberry can be substituted for the lime jelly.

3 tablespoons water
3 cubes (approx. ¼ slab) lime jelly
75–100 ml (3–4 fl oz) vanilla ice cream
4 tablespoons double cream

0.55 litre (1 pint) jug

Put the 3 tablespoons water in an 0.55 litre (1 pint) jug and cook, without covering, on Full Power for 1 minute or until boiling.

Add the jelly cubes, stir for a few seconds to start the dissolving process, then cook, without covering, on Full Power for 30 seconds. Stir thoroughly until the jelly is completely dissolved, then leave to cool but not set.

In a bowl soften the ice cream with a fork, add the double cream and beat with a wire whisk until the mixture doubles in volume and a soft peak will just hold its shape when the whisk is lifted from the mixture.

Thoroughly beat the cooled but still liquid jelly into the thickened cream, then pour into a stemmed glass. Cover and leave in a cool place to set.

RICE PUDDING

This pudding becomes creamier as it cools and it reheats successfully. Should you wish to eat it immediately after cooking, add a further 5–10 minutes to the cooking time.

25 g (1 oz) pudding rice
15 g (½ oz) caster sugar
15 g (½ oz) butter
300 ml (½ pint) milk
¼ teaspoon grated nutmeg

1.95 litre (3½ pint) bowl

Put all the ingredients into a 1.95 litre (3½ pint) bowl and cook, without covering, on Full Power for 3½ minutes or until the mixture boils. Stir thoroughly.

Cover with the cling film, pulling back one corner to vent, and cook on the Defrost (30 per cent) setting for 17–20 minutes or until the rice is tender.

STEWED DRIED FRUIT

This is best served cold. A 24-hour rest in a cool place will result in softer fruit and a thicker syrup.

> 100 g (4 oz) (approx. a handful) mixed prunes, dried
>   apricots, dried peaches, dried apple rings or a
>   selection of any of these
> 250 ml (8 fl oz) hot water (approx.)
> 2 level tablespoons demerara sugar
>
> 0.55 litre (1 pint) jug

Put the fruit into an 0.55 litre (1 pint) jug and add just sufficient water to cover the fruit. Cook, without covering, on Full Power for 3 minutes or until the water boils.

Stir in the sugar and cook, without covering, on Full Power for 5 minutes, stirring once during cooking.

Stir, cover and leave to cool.

Jams and Curds

Jams retain more colour when prepared in small quantities and this is just as well, for (as would be the case for a single person) it is monotonous to have to eat the same type of jam day after day until the jar is empty. With this recipe, you can make one small jarful at a time. If you are addicted to jam, you could have three different kinds in a week.

The smaller the quantity the faster is the cooking time and 250 g (8 oz) is ready in under 10 minutes. Marmalade is better, however, when cooked in a larger quantity and that is why no recipe is included here.

Use frozen or fresh fruit, choosing the best fruits for 'jelling'. These include gooseberries, plums, blackcurrants, blackberries and raspberries. Don't use more than an amount of sugar equal to the weight of the fruit and stop cooking as soon as a drop of the liquid clings to the edge of a spoon. Always cook in a heat-proof bowl large enough to contain the syrup as it rises.

Fruits with very thin skins need no added water, but tougher-skinned berries such as blackcurrants do – they should be cooked until tender before stirring in the sugar.

The most popular of the curds is lemon, but orange or grapefruit make a very pleasant change. Frozen or canned juice can be substituted for fresh. Be sure to stir frequently during cooking to avoid curdling.

THE RECIPES

Apricot Preserve
Blackcurrant Jam
Lemon Curd

APRICOT PRESERVE

To heat a jam jar, put in sufficient water to reach 2.5 cm (1 in) up the jar and heat in the microwave on Full Power until bubbling. Pour off the water and fill with the freshly cooked jam.

225 g (8 oz) dried apricots
450 ml (¾ pint) hot water
2 teaspoons lemon juice
175 g (6 oz) caster sugar

1.95 litre (3½ pint) bowl

Finely chop the apricots and put into a 1.95 litre (3½ pint) bowl with the water and lemon juice. Three-quarters cover with cling film and cook on Full Power for 10–12 minutes, stirring twice during cooking, until the fruit is soft.

Remove the bowl from the microwave and stir in the sugar. Cook, without covering, for 2 minutes, then stir until the sugar has dissolved. Cook, still uncovered, for a further 6–8 minutes until the mixture is very thick. Pour into a heated jar and cover with cling film or a jam pot cover.

Makes about 450 g (1 lb).

BLACKCURRANT JAM

It is essential to cook the blackcurrants in the water until
the skins are soft (before adding the sugar) or the skins
will toughen. Blackcurrant jam sets very firmly so do not
overcook.

  225 g (8 oz) blackcurrants
  4 tablespoons water
  225 g (8 oz) granulated sugar
  1 teaspoon fresh lemon juice

  1.95 litre (3½ pint) ovenglass bowl

Put the blackcurrants and water into a 1.95 litre (3½
pint) ovenglass bowl, three-quarters cover with cling film
and cook on Full Power for 5 minutes or until the skins
are soft.

Remove the cling film, stir in the sugar and lemon
juice and cook, without covering, on Full Power for 9–11
minutes, stirring once during the early part of cooking.
Begin testing after 9 minutes' cooking time, stirring with
a wooden spoon. The jam is ready when droplets of it fall
slowly off the wooden spoon.

Pot the jam in a warmed jar or pour into a dish. Leave
until cold before using.

Makes 225 g (½ lb).

LEMON CURD

Lemon curd does not keep very well so should be kept in
a cool place and consumed within a week.

  50 g (2 oz) unsalted butter
  5 tablespoons fresh (not bottled) lemon juice (approx.
    2 lemons)

100 g (4 oz) caster sugar
2 eggs, beaten and threads removed

1 litre (1¾ pint) bowl
Jam jar

Put the butter into a 1 litre (1¾ pint) bowl and cook, without covering, on Full Power for 30 seconds or until melted.

Stir in the lemon juice and sugar and add the eggs. Stir thoroughly and cook, without covering, on Full Power for 2 minutes, beating with a wire whisk every 30 seconds. As soon as thickening appears around the edges, test with the whisk to see if the mixture has attained the texture of softly whipped cream. Cook for up to a further 30 seconds, beating once during this time.

Remove the bowl from the microwave and beat for 2 minutes. Pour into a heated jar or dish and leave until cold. Cover with a lid.

Breakfasts, Snacks, Drinks and Sauces

This is a chapter that includes a collection of basic recipes and bits and pieces that didn't seem to fit in anywhere else. Eggs, for example, can be eaten at any time – as part of a main course, for breakfast or in sandwiches. Sauces are equally versatile.

All kinds of warm drinks can be prepared in the microwave usually in a cup or mug. Air bubbles in water increase in size during heating and explode when boiling continues for too long. Stir gently before microwaving or lightly tap the filled container on the work surface.

Milk will rise up and over which means that milky drinks should not be allowed to boil. How many times has this happened to you when heating milk conventionally in a saucepan on the hob? The microwave setting on an oven with variable control can be turned down as can the controls on the hob. Similarly, opening the microwave door will arrest the heating process as does taking the pan off the hob.

Leave liquids to cool for a few seconds before adding sugar and milk, and stir before drinking to be sure of an even temperature throughout.

Hot wine remains a popular winter beverage and when you have finally succumbed to a head cold you can prepare your hot toddy in the microwave. Summer drinks – initially cooked for serving cold – may be prepared just as easily and these can include iced tea, iced coffee and cold punch.

If conventional sauce-making is a nightmare, preparing it in the microwave is a dream. Microwaved white sauces are never lumpy and emulsified sauces are easier to cook, although you still have to keep a watchful eye to avoid a curdle.

The microwave oven is so useful for all the minor cooking chores, like melting chocolate, drying herbs, melting gelatine (even liquefying soap scraps etc), all tricky jobs to do conventionally. (I would welcome any suggestions you may have as we all learn something new every day.)

THE RECIPES

Bacon
Baked Beans on Toast
Basic White Sauce
Boiled Eggs
Burgers
Cocoa
Crispies
Croûtons
Crumbed Chicken
Custard (made with Custard Powder)
Easy Bread Sauce
Easy-Cook Pizza
Espagnole Sauce
Fish Fingers and crumbed Fish Fillets

French Toast
Fried Egg in a Browning Dish
Frozen Commercial Pizza
Hollandaise Sauce
Melting Chocolate
Poached Egg (1) and (2)
Porridge
Prawn Vol-au-Vent
Quick and Easy Browned Crumbs
Sausages
Scrambled Eggs
Stocks
Toasted Almonds
Toasted Sandwiches
Traditional Bread Sauce

BACON

The quickest way to cook bacon is to place the rashers side by side on one half of a piece of kitchen paper and fold the other half over the bacon, making sure that any pattern on the paper is facing outwards. Place in the microwave on Full Power and allow 30 seconds for one rasher or 45 seconds for 2 rashers cooked together. Immediately remove the bacon rashers from the paper (this will have absorbed the surplus fat).

To cook the bacon on a plate, ready to serve straight from the oven, put the bacon rashers side by side, cover with a piece of kitchen paper (undecorated surface against the rashers) and allow a similar cooking time.

To cook browned and crispy bacon you need a browning dish. Preheat the empty dish for 2 minutes, add the bacon rashers and cook, without covering, for 30 seconds. Flip the rashers over and move them around the dish with tongs, then add any extra cooking time necessary.

BAKED BEANS ON TOAST

The beans can be heated on the toast, but this tends to make the latter soggy, so make the toast while heating the beans in the microwave.

Open the can and pour as many beans as you want into a suitable cereal bowl or jug. Cover with vented cling film and heat on Full Power for 1–2 minutes or until the beans are bubbling around the edges. Carefully remove the cling film, stir the beans, then cook, without covering, for a further 30 seconds.

BASIC WHITE SAUCE

You *must* master the art of sauce-making as sauces are so versatile. Make them thin for pouring, thicker for coating and very thick if needed for a soufflé intended to be cooked in the conventional way. Add appropriate seasonings to complement the food you are serving – grated cheese, chopped parsley, saffron, mashed anchovies and chopped hard-boiled egg are just a few suggestions. Use fish, chicken or vegetable stock instead of milk to give your sauces added flavour.

To accompany puddings and ice cream, you can use flavourings such as honey, sugar, puréed fruit or chocolate.

For 150 ml (¼ pint) pouring sauce you need:
2 level teaspoons butter or margarine, or 1 tablespoon oil
2 level teaspoons flour
150 ml (¼ pint) milk

For 150 ml (¼ pint) coating sauce you need:
1 level tablespoon butter or margarine, or 2 tablespoons oil
2 level tablespoons flour
150 ml (¼ pint) milk

For a very thick sauce (panada) you need:
2 level tablespoons butter or margarine, or 4 tablespoons oil
4 level tablespoons flour
150ml (¼ pint) milk

Method:
Because of the small quantity involved, the all-in-one method of making the sauce is easiest. Double the quantities and increase the timings for 300 ml (½ pint) sauce.

For sauce made with butter or margarine, put the fat in the bowl and heat on Full Power for 20 seconds or until melted. Stir in the flour and milk and cook, without covering, on Full Power for 1 minute. Beat with a wire whisk. Cook for a further 30 seconds, whisk again, then cook for a final 30 seconds and once more thoroughly whisk. Add your chosen flavourings.

To make the sauce with oil combine all the ingredients and cook, without covering, on Full Power for 2 minutes, beating every 30 seconds.

BOILED EGGS

Almost everyone will tell you that eggs cannot be cooked in their shells in the microwave because they will burst. However, with a little skilful conjuring, eggs can be boiled successfully in this fashion. The use of foil prevents the microwaves from penetrating and the water, which is kept at boiling point by the microwaves, cooks the eggs in the usual way.

1, 2 or 3 eggs
Aluminium foil
Boiling water

Medium size jug or bowl

Wrap each egg completely in smooth foil, finishing with a twist on top. Put the egg 'parcels' into a medium-size jug or bowl.

Pour the boiling water over the eggs until it covers the packets and reaches three-quarters up the sides of the jug or bowl. Cook, without covering, on Full Power for 3–4 minutes for soft eggs and 12–15 minutes for hard-boiled eggs.

Remove the jug carefully from the microwave and take out the egg parcels with a slotted spoon or tongs. Put them on a cloth to absorb any drips of water. Carefully unwrap the eggs and discard the foil.

BURGERS

Cook burgers from frozen on a plate or in a browning dish.

Commercial burgers are usually thin and somewhat fatty – the microwave draws out the fat, removing all those unwanted calories.

Home-made burgers can be shaped to suit your preference and if you make them on the thicker side (approx. 1.25–2 cm (¼ to ¾ in)) you will find them less tough than the purchased types.

In the cooking, all burgers tend to assume an oval shape and they will brown whether or not you use a browning dish. The colour change occurs gradually over a period of 3 minutes. *Beware – overcooked burgers become too leathery to eat.*

Frozen burger on a plate:
Put the burger on kitchen paper on a plate. Cover with another piece of kitchen paper and cook on Full Power for 45–60 seconds. Allow 1½–2 minutes for two burgers cooked at the same time. As soon as the burgers are ready remove the kitchen paper which will have absorbed the surplus fat.

Burger in the browning dish:
Place the burger on kitchen paper and place in the microwave. Heat on Full Power for 20 seconds just sufficiently to take off the chill. Remove the burger and paper.

Preheat the empty unlidded browning dish for 3 minutes. Immediately press the burger on to the hot surface, then turn over to brown the other side. Cook, without covering, on Full Power for 30 seconds.

To cook two burgers, sandwich them together and

pretend they are one – allow an extra 15 seconds' cooking time and serve browned side up.

Burgers can be cooked from frozen in the browning dish but will not achieve quite so much browning. They must be cooked one at a time, reheating the dish for 30 seconds before cooking the second one.

Home-made burgers are easy to prepare but you must start with raw lean mince. It is preferable to allow frozen mince to thaw slowly in the refrigerator, but if necessary it can be thawed in the dish, uncovered, with the microwave set at the 10 per cent or No. 1 (Warm or Hold) setting. Home-made burgers can be varied by adding grated cheese, breadcrumbs or chopped bacon.

Single Burger:
100 g (4 oz) lean minced beef
Small piece onion, grated or very finely chopped (or
  onion seasoning)
Salt
Pepper
Left-over beaten egg, if available

Mix the beef and seasoning together and bind with beaten egg, if available. Shape into a 7.5 cm (3 in) round patty.

Put on a plate, cover with kitchen paper and cook for 45–60 seconds on Full Power. Two burgers cooked together will take 1½–2 minutes.

Leave to stand for 2–3 minutes before eating.

COCOA

½–1 level teaspoon cocoa powder
4 tablespoons cold water
6 tablespoons milk
Sugar to taste

Suitable mug

Stir together the cocoa powder and water in a suitable glass or cup and heat, without covering, on Full Power for 30 seconds.

Add the milk, stir gently with a fork, and then heat, uncovered, on Full Power for 1 minute. Add sugar to taste and stir before drinking.

CRISPIES

A way to use up bread crusts if you have used the soft inside of the loaf for making breadcrumbs. Save and store the crusts in the freezer until you have a small collection, then cook in this simple way in the microwave to provide you with nibbles to eat while waiting for your meal.

Crusts from 4 slices bread (thawed, if stored in the freezer)
25 g (1 oz) butter or margarine

0.4 litre (¾ pint) oval pie dish

If you have not already done so cut the crusts into sticks.

Put the butter in an 0.4 litre (¾ pint) oval pie dish and heat on Full Power for 30–60 seconds or until melted.

Mix in the crusts and cook, without covering, on Full Power for 2–3 minutes, stirring once or twice, until the bread sticks are crisp but not brown. Use oven gloves to remove the dish from the microwave.

CROÛTONS

For a variation add a shake of garlic salt or a crushed garlic clove or 1 level teaspoon grated Parmesan cheese to the oil.

2 slices bread
2 tablespoons vegetable oil
¼–½ level teaspoon paprika

21.5 cm (8½ in) round pie dish

Remove the crusts and cut the bread into small dice.

Put the oil into a 21.5 cm (8½ in) round pie dish and heat on Full Power for 1–2 minutes. Stir in the paprika and any other flavourings.

Add the bread to the dish, tossing the dice so that they are completely coated in the flavoured oil. Cook, without covering, on Full Power for 3–4 minutes, stirring frequently until the croûtons are golden brown. (Do not overcook or the croûtons will burn.) Drain on absorbent kitchen paper.

CRUMBED CHICKEN

This is something that you can prepare yourself by simply dipping the skinned raw chicken in seasoned beaten egg and then coating with golden breadcrumbs. A single chicken breast should not take more than 1 minute on each side to cook, with the oven on Full Power and the chicken covered with non-stick paper.

Note: You *must not* deep fry (and cannot properly shallow fry) in the microwave and you cannot cook battered chicken or fish.

CUSTARD (MADE WITH CUSTARD POWDER)

Most people have a tin or a few packets of custard powder tucked away in the cupboard. However, if none is available you can substitute cornflour with the addition of a little vanilla essence and a drop or two of orange food colouring.

Custard is best made with full-cream milk but liquid skimmed milk produces a very acceptable result. Should you only have dried milk, either full cream or skimmed, you can add the correct quantity of powder or granules for 150 ml (¼ pint) made-up milk to the custard powder and sugar, then make up with 150 ml (¼ pint) water.

1 level tablespoon custard powder
½ level tablespoon sugar
150 ml (¼ pint) milk

0.55 litre (1 pint) jug

Mix the custard powder, sugar and a little of the cold milk in an 0.55 litre (1 pint) jug or bowl.

Gradually stir in the remainder of the milk, then cook on Full Power for 2 minutes. Stir every 30 seconds to prevent the custard from boiling over. If possible use a wire whisk for stirring (although this will be quite difficult if you are cooking the custard in a jug). Custard thickens during cooling but if, when you have finished cooking, you are not satisfied and feel that the custard is too thin, you may continue the cooking for a further 30 seconds.

EASY BREAD SAUCE

This quick method uses only ground spices and herbs, enabling the flavour to develop more quickly.

1½ slices white bread, crusts removed
9 tablespoons milk
Small slice onion, skinned and finely chopped
Pinch ground mace
Pinch bayleaf powder
Pinch ground cloves

White pepper
Salt
Pea-sized knob of butter

1 litre (1¾ pint) bowl

Put the slice of bread into a 1 litre (1¾ pint) bowl and
spoon the milk over. Allow a few moments for the bread
to soften and when it is completely soaked, beat in the
other ingredients, using a fork.

Cook, without covering, on Full Power for 2 minutes,
watching carefully as the mixture will boil up towards the
end of the cooking period. Beat vigorously with a wire
whisk.

Return the bowl to the microwave, reduce the setting
to Defrost (30 per cent) and cook for 2–3 minutes,
whisking at the end of the cooking time.

EASY-COOK PIZZA

We feel we have made a real breakthrough with this
recipe in which the base is cooked freshly but separately
from the topping. We have also tried reheating a left-
over piece, placing it on a rack to prevent it becoming
soft underneath, and it was surprisingly good. Pizzas
invariably have a topping which consists of tomatoes and
cheese to which other ingredients are added. You can
use any topping which will reheat successfully in the
microwave but for the best results, the topping should be
cooked first so that it is ready to spread on the freshly
baked base. Cheese melts very quickly indeed in the
microwave and overcooking causes it to become stringy.

Basic Pizza Topping

7 g (¼ oz) butter
1 small onion, peeled and grated

½ level teaspoon cornflour
½ small can tomatoes
¼ level teaspoon dried oregano
Freshly ground black pepper
25 g (1 oz) grated Cheddar cheese
Few canned anchovy fillets (drained) or cooked strips bacon; stuffed green olives or pitted black olives to garnish

1.95 litre (3½ pint) bowl

Put the butter in a 1.95 litre (3½ pint) bowl and heat, without covering, on Full Power for 15 seconds or until melted. Stir in the onion and cook for 2 minutes. Blend in the cornflour then add the canned tomatoes (but not the juice), the oregano and pepper to taste. Cook, uncovered, for 2–3 minutes, stirring occasionally until the mixture bubbles. Keep hot until the pizza base is cooked.

Easy-Cook Pizza Base

100 g (4 oz) self-raising flour
½ level teaspoon baking powder
Pinch salt
25 g (1 oz) butter or margarine
½ beaten egg
2 tablespoons milk
Knob of butter

20 cm (8 in) browning dish

Sieve the flour, baking powder and salt into a bowl, add the butter cut into several pieces, then rub in with the fingertips until the mixture is like fine crumbs.

Mix together the egg and milk, pour on to the flour mixture and stir gently with a fork until a very soft dough is formed.

Scoop the dough on to a lightly floured surface and knead very gently until it is just smooth, then press or roll into a 15 cm (6 in) circle.

Preheat a 20 cm (8 in) browning dish for about 3 minutes, then add a knob of butter – this should sizzle and brown if the dish is sufficiently hot. Holding the handle carefully with an oven mitt, tip the browning dish so that the entire surface becomes lightly covered with a film of the butter.

Quickly put in the pizza base; press down once, firmly, with a fish slice, then flip the dough over and cook, without covering, on Full Power for 2 minutes. You will probably see the dough balloon up and when this happens, flip it over once more.

Spoon the hot topping on to the pizza base (leaving the base still in the browning dish) and spread the topping to within 1 cm (½ in) of the edge. Sprinkle the cheese on top, then decorate with either anchovy fillets or bacon strips, and olives.

Either leave the pizza in the browning dish or transfer to a serving plate and reheat, uncovered, on Full Power for 1–1½ minutes, which should be just sufficient to heat the topping.

ESPAGNOLE SAUCE

The oil and flour mixture becomes very hot during cooking, so that you must use a bowl or dish that is completely heat resistant. Wear oven gloves to transfer the bowl to a dry heatproof surface. I have used Pyrex and Denby successfully, but none of the various plastic bowls were suitable. This recipe both refrigerates and freezes satisfactorily.

2 tablespoons salad oil
2 level tablespoons plain flour
1 slice onion, peeled and finely chopped
½ celery stalk, finely chopped
1 rasher lean bacon, trimmed of all rind and fat, then
  chopped
1 small carrot, scraped and grated
1 level teaspoon freshly chopped parsley
1 bay leaf
Salt
Freshly ground black pepper
1 level teaspoon tomato purée
2 tablespoons medium red wine
300 ml (½ pint) strong hot beef stock, or 300 ml
  (½ pint) boiling water and one stock cube, crumbled

1 litre (1¾ pint) bowl

Stir the oil and flour together in a 1 litre (1¾ pint) bowl,
then cook, without covering, on Full Power for 3½–4
minutes or until the flour starts to brown. Occasionally
you will see a patch of burnt flour which should be stirred
in immediately; this will equalize the colour. Stir once
after cooking.

Mix in the onion and celery stalk and cook, without
covering, on Full Power for 1 minute.

Add the chopped bacon, stirring well and cook,
uncovered, for a further 30 seconds. Add the remaining
ingredients, three-quarters cover the bowl with cling film
and cook on Full Power for 5 minutes.

Remove the bay leaf and liquidize the mixture. Return
the sauce to the bowl, reduce the setting and reheat on
Defrost (30 per cent) for 5 minutes.

Makes about 300 ml (½ pint)

FISH FINGERS AND CRUMBED FISH FILLETS

These can be cooked in the microwave, but unless a browning dish is used, they will not be crisp. Unless cooked in oil they will not change colour at all. At a pinch you can put the fish on a plate, arranging fish fingers in a circle. If cooking from frozen allow 10–20 seconds per fish finger on Full Power. To cook frozen crumbed fillets give 3 minutes on Defrost (30 per cent) followed by 1–2 minutes on Full Power.

A better method is to put a tablespoon of oil in a shallow dish, heat on Full Power for 1 minute, put the fish fingers or fillet (best side down) in the oil, and allow the same times as above. Turn the fish over once during the cooking period.

For really crispy results pre-heat a browning dish for the manufacturer's recommended time, add 2 teaspoons oil, press the fish down on to the hot surface and cook, without covering, on Full Power for 30 seconds. Turn the fish over and continue cooking on Full Power – for 4 fingers allow another 15 seconds; for a 150 g (6 oz) fillet allow 2–2½ minutes in all.

FRENCH TOAST

Since the microwave cannot brown it is not possible to use it for making toast. Nevertheless if no grill or toaster is available, French Toast can be made in the microwave in a browning dish. To make more than a single piece, first butter each slice of bread on both sides and place on a sheet of non-stick paper so that the butter does not adhere to the work surface.

Put the unlidded browning dish in the microwave and heat at Full Power for 3 minutes. Immediately press a slice of the prepared bread into the hot browning dish and cook, without covering, for 15 seconds. Flip the bread over, press down with a fish slice and cook for a further 10 seconds. Serve at once.

To toast another slice reheat the empty unrinsed dish for 30 seconds, then cook as before.

Reheat the empty dish before toasting a further slice.

Note: You cannot consecutively make more than 3 slices of French Toast in this way. Overheating of the browning dish may cause the glass or ceramic microwave shelf or turntable to break – the dish itself will not.

FRIED EGG IN A BROWNING DISH

This is a really good way of frying eggs in the microwave and the eggs will cook best if a small browning dish is used.

1–2 eggs
Knob of butter

Small browning dish with lid

Preheat the empty browning dish in the microwave oven on Full Power for 3 minutes. Add the butter and if it sizzles and browns, quickly break in the eggs. Should the dish not be hot enough, preheat for a further minute before adding the eggs.

Immediately cover the dish with the lid or a plate, return the dish to the microwave oven and cook on Full Power for 20–30 seconds only. Leave to stand for 30 seconds before serving.

Note: When you are a beginning at frying eggs in the microwave, you may prefer to prick the yolk first as any overcooking would cause it to burst.

FROZEN COMMERCIAL PIZZA

There is nothing to stop you from heating a frozen pizza in the microwave oven by placing the pizza on a piece of kitchen paper or a plate and cooking on Full Power until the pizza is hot, but it does not produce the best results.

The best way of heating is by means of a browning dish, so you must buy a pizza that will fit into your particular dish. The very tiny ones are usually suitable for the small saucepan-type browning dish and can of course be cooked in any of the larger-sized dishes, but if you are going to cook larger pizzas you have to make sure that you have a large enough browning dish. The small browning dish will take an 11 cm (4½ in) pizza; the 20 cm (8 in) dish will take a 17.5 cm (7 in) pizza; while the large browning dish takes a 22.5 cm (9 in) pizza. There are also special pizza browning dishes available but they are not essential – they perform the same function.

Pre-heat the empty browning dish for 1 minute less than the manufacturer recommends, and meanwhile have butter, a knife and tongs at the ready.

As soon as the microwave switches off, open the door, put a knob of butter into the empty dish, spreading it around with the knife to coat the entire base. Put the pizza in the dish, cheesy side down, and hold it there with the back of the tongs for 20 seconds. Immediately flip the pizza over, base-side down, and cook on Full Power for 2 minutes.

Put the lid on the dish, cook on Full Power for 1 minute, then remove the lid and cook on Full Power for a further minute. Serve at once.

It is difficult to give an exact pre-heating time; that given above is correct if the pizza is well and truly frozen. However, if it has been left to stand in the kitchen, or is being cooked after bringing it back from the shop, it will be less frozen and you will need to reduce the pre-heating time by 1 minute and the cooking time by about 30 seconds. If the dish is too hot, the pizza will be inclined to burn underneath – although I think it is rather tasty done that way.

HOLLANDAISE SAUCE

The microwave method is different from the usual way which requires a double saucepan and in which the butter is added last.

Use a small bowl because its narrow diameter helps the sauce to cook more evenly, and beat frequently as curdling starts around the edges (this is the area which is heated first in the microwave).

There are many different recipes for making Hollandaise sauce. Cream can be mixed in when adding the egg; fresh orange or fresh lime juice give delicate flavour; and the quantity of liquid can be increased when a thinner sauce is desired.

The egg white, beaten until soft peaks form, can be folded into the warm sauce to produce a thin fluffy mousseuse sauce.

50 g (2 oz) butter
2 teaspoons fresh lemon juice
1 egg yolk
Salt
Pepper

0.55 litre (1 pint) jug

Cut up the butter and put into an 0.55 litre (1 pint) jug. Heat, without covering, on Full Power for 30 seconds or until melted.

Add the lemon juice and then the egg yolk and stir briskly with a fork.

Cook, without covering, on Defrost (30 per cent) for 1½ minutes, beating every 30 seconds, until the sauce thickens.

Season to taste with salt and pepper and beat vigorously.

MELTING CHOCOLATE

Chocolate can be used as cake decoration or in hot drinks and, of course, cold milk shakes. Chocolate can also be used in pudding mixes; as a simple sauce; or poured over ice cream.

Melt chocolate on non-stick paper or in a suitable small jug, bowl or dish. Use as much as you require and leave any surplus in the container. When cold, scrape out the hardened chocolate with a sharp knife and save for the next time, or finely chop to use as decoration.

25–50 g (1–2 oz) plain dessert or block cooking
  chocolate

Remove the wrapping and make sure that no fragments of the foil cling to the chocolate.

Break into pieces and put into the chosen container. Heat, without covering, on Full Power for 1 minute or until a sheen appears on the chocolate pieces. (The shape may not have changed.)

Stir with a table knife, then continue heating and stirring every 15 seconds until the melted chocolate is smooth. The total melting time will be between 1½ and 2½ minutes.

POACHED EGGS (1)

Individual microwave-suitable poachers are obtainable
and these produce a nice poached-egg shape. Eggs can
also be poached in a suitable cup or ramekin. The most
foolproof way is to cook them in a lightly greased dish or
ramekin. They can also be cooked in water (see following
recipe) but this method tends to cause pitting in the egg
white.

Grease the individual dishes and add the shelled egg.
Cover loosely with cling film, place on the turntable or
shelf and cook on the Defrost (30 per cent) setting for
about 2 minutes or until the yolk is just set.

When cooking more than one egg in this way, arrange
the dishes in a circle in the microwave oven; when
cooking a single egg the dish can be placed in the centre.
It is a matter of personal preference as to how long they
should be cooked, but two eggs will take about 3 minutes
and four eggs about 4 minutes.

POACHED EGGS (2)

To poach eggs safely in water in the microwave, use a
cereal bowl or basin so that there is plenty of room for
the water to bubble around the edges and for the steam
to escape.

  150–300 ml (¼–½ pint) boiling water
  Pinch salt
  1 egg

  1 cereal bowl or basin

To cook a single egg, half-fill the cereal bowl with boiling
water and add the salt. Put the bowl in the microwave

oven and heat, without covering, on Full Power until the water is boiling rapidly.

Swirl the water with the handle of a wooden spoon to create a whirlpool effect. Break the egg into the centre, partly cover with cling film, reduce the setting to Medium (50 per cent) and cook for 1 minute. Leave for a few moments, then remove the cling film carefully and transfer the egg to a plate with the aid of a slotted spoon.

To cook two eggs, boil and salt the water, swirl with the aid of the wooden spoon, break in one egg and cook on Full Power for 30 seconds. Add the second egg and microwave on Full Power for a further 30 seconds.

To cook three eggs, use a bowl or basin of larger diameter and break in the eggs one at a time, first swirling the water with the wooden spoon handle. Three eggs will take about 1½ minutes to cook.

PORRIDGE

Porridge will keep for two or three days if covered and refrigerated, but during this time it does tend to thicken up. This recipe is for a single portion but if you double or treble the recipe, remember that you need to use a much larger bowl.

3 level tablespoons porridge oats
5 tablespoons milk
5 tablespoons water
Salt
Sugar to taste

Cereal bowl

Mix the oats, milk, water and salt together in a cereal bowl and cook without covering, on Full Power for 1½ minutes. Stir thoroughly.

Reduce the setting to Defrost (30 per cent) and cook, uncovered, for 1½–2½ minutes.

Stir before eating, adding sugar to taste.

PRAWN VOL-AU-VENT

Some bakers sell ready-baked vol-au-vent cases. It is best to put them into a hot conventional oven for a few minutes to become crisp, before adding the hot filling. Frozen individual vol-au-vent cases store well and these can be cooked in the microwave.

Vary the fillings, using cooked chicken, canned tuna or salmon, raw scallops or sliced mushrooms. Add cooked fillings towards the end of the cooking time; add raw ingredients as soon as the sauce thickens and cook for a little longer.

> 3 × 6–6¾ cm (2½–3 in) frozen vol-au-vent cases, left
>   at room temperature for 10 minutes to commence
>   thawing
> 1 tablespoon salad oil
> 1 level tablespoon flour
> 5 tablespoons milk
> 1 level teaspoon tomato ketchup
> Salt
> Pepper
> 50 g (2 oz) thawed cooked prawns, chopped
>
> 0.55 ml (1 pint) bowl

First cook the sauce. Put the oil, flour, milk and ketchup into an 0.55 ml (1 pint) bowl and mix thoroughly with a wire whisk. Cook, without covering, on Full Power for 30 seconds, whisk and cook for a further 30 seconds. Season to taste.

Stir in the prawns and cook for 1 minute, stirring once

during and once after cooking. Cover and set aside while cooking the vol-au-vent cases.

Put the vol-au-vent in a circle on a piece of kitchen paper (white side up if using the decorated kind). Cook, without covering, on Full Power for 2–3 minutes until the pastry holds its risen shape and does not flop when the oven door is opened. Sometimes the pastry rises unevenly; in this situation, it is often possible to reshape it during cooking using a round-bladed knife.

Quickly brown the tops of the cases under the grill if you really feel this to be necessary, then fill with the prawn mixture. Slightly overfill each case so that the mixture runs over the edges of the pastry to hide its pallor.

Microwaved puff pastry tastes the same as when baked conventionally – it is only the appearance that is different.

QUICK AND EASY BROWNED CRUMBS

Use any bowl or shallow dish to cook these crumbs provided that it is made of a material that is resistant to the very high temperature that the crumbs will reach. Ovenglass or oven-to-table pottery is generally suitable.

1 slice bread, crusts removed
2 tablespoons vegetable oil

Finely chop the bread. The easiest way is to cut very thin strips one way, then gather these together and slice them finely the other way. The crumbs will not be very fine but this is an easy way to prepare them, dispensing with the need to use a grater, liquidizer or food processor.

Mix the crumbs and the oil in the dish and cook, without covering, on Full Power for 4–5 minutes or until the crumbs are golden. Stir once or twice during cooking to prevent burning.

Carefully remove the dish from the microwave using oven gloves and drain the crumbs on kitchen paper.

Use as a garnish for vegetables or soups.

SAUSAGES

You can cook sausages in several ways – either entirely by microwave or using the microwave in conjunction with the grill or frying pan. They can be cooked from frozen or be defrosted first in the microwave.

Cheap sausages usually have a higher fat content and these are the kind that are likely to burst. Better-quality sausages can often be cooked without prior pricking, but otherwise always prick – although when the sausages are separated from each other, the ends, now being unsealed, may be sufficiently open to allow for expansion as the sausage cooks so that pricking will not necessary.

Thawing:
To thaw a sausage in the microwave place it on the oven shelf or a suitable plate and allow 1–2 minutes on the Defrost (30 per cent) setting.

Cooking sausages on a plate:
To cook a frozen sausage in the microwave without browning put it on a plate, cover with kitchen paper and cook on Defrost (30 per cent) for about 2 minutes. Turn the sausage over, replace the paper and cook for a further 3–4 minutes. If the sausage appears to be darkening this is a sign of overcooking. Two frozen sausages cooked together in the same way will take about 10 minutes, and you should turn them over after 4 minutes.

To cook a thawed sausage without browning prick the sausage, put on a suitable plate, cover with kitchen paper and cook on Full Power for 2 minutes. Turn the sausage over, replace the kitchen paper and cook for a further 1–1½ minutes.

Brown the sausages in a frying pan or under a preheated grill.

Sausages can be thawed in the microwave and then cooked entirely in the conventional way, or you can par-cook them in the microwave which will then shorten the conventional cooking time.

Cooking sausages in a browning dish:
To cook a thawed sausage and brown it, use a browning dish. Prick the sausage well. Preheat the unlidded dish on Full Power for 3 minutes, add a knob of butter, swirl the dish (using oven gloves) and put the sausage in the dish and then flip it over using tongs. Cook, without covering, on Full Power for about 2 minutes, turning the sausage over half-way through cooking.

To cook two sausages in this way, follow the same procedure, allowing an extra 30–60 seconds cooking time.

Cooking sausage and bacon in a browning dish:
To cook sausage and bacon in the browning dish add the bacon rashers 30 seconds before the end of the cooking time for the sausages. If you wish you can also add an egg immediately the bacon is ready. Place the lid on the dish and leave to stand for 20–30 seconds without further cooking (the residual heat will cook the egg). Transfer the food to a hot serving plate (this can be warmed by dipping into very hot water).

A few mushrooms put into the hot unrinsed browning dish and cooked on Full Power will take only 1 more minute. If you then wish to add a halved tomato, allow a further 30 seconds' cooking to complete your full English breakfast.

SCRAMBLED EGG

The secret here is to cook the eggs in a jug or large cup. They are not nearly so good when cooked on a plate. It is important to remember that scrambled eggs continue to cook and harden after the microwave is switched off and this is especially the case if the eggs are left in the cooking container. (This also happens in a pan on the conventional hob.) Extra heating time can always be added just before serving, if the toast is not ready.

1–2 eggs
1–2 tablespoons milk
Salt
Pepper
Small knob of butter

Jug

Break the egg(s) into the jug; add the milk and season to taste.

Beat lightly with a fork, then add the butter which will not melt at this stage.

Cook, without covering, on Full Power for 30 seconds, then stir vigorously up and down – not round and round – to mix the partly set egg with the liquid that remains in the middle. Continue cooking, stirring every 15–30 seconds, until the egg is just set.

For a more filling meal add diced ham, grated cheese, cooked prawns or diced cooked vegetables to the egg mixture before cooking, adding extra time if necessary.

STOCKS

Chicken and fish stocks are so easy to make in the microwave.

Chicken Stock: Put the cut-up chicken carcass, skin etc in a 2.8 litre (5 pint) bowl, add water to cover and include a small piece of onion, carrot and a bay leaf. Three-quarters cover with cling film and cook on Full Power for 35 minutes.

Fish Stock: Put roughly cut bones and skin (left-overs will do if you are going to use the stock for yourself) into a 1 litre (1¾ pint) bowl. Add water just to cover together with seasonings and cook, without covering, on Full Power until the liquid boils. Immediately reduce the setting to Defrost (30 per cent) and cook for a further 10–15 minutes.

TOASTED ALMONDS

You can double or treble the quantity of almonds given here but you must remember to stir frequently and extend the cooking time. The cooled almonds can be stored for some time in a screw-top jar.

  25 g (1 oz) flaked almonds
  Non-stick paper circle

Place the flaked almonds on the non-stick paper in the microwave oven and cook on Full Power for 3–4 minutes, stirring frequently with the fingers, until the nuts are pale brown. A few of the nuts may darken quickly and in this case they should be removed immediately.

  Make sure that the almonds are not heaped together in clusters as this increases the chance of burning.

TOASTED SANDWICHES

A browning dish is a must for preparing toasted sandwiches in the microwave. You will need to make sure that a slice of the bread you choose will fit into that browning dish. It is difficult to recommend a preheating time, but about half the maximum cooking time recommended by the manufacturer is usually sufficient to obtain a good brown crisp toast. Choose cheese, ham, salami (or a combination) or canned fish for the filling and cook one sandwich at a time. If you require a second one, there is no need to wipe out the dish but it should nevertheless be reheated for 1 minute before proceeding.

2 slices (of matching size) day-old bread, buttered on what will be the outside
25–50 g (1–2 oz) grated or sliced cheese, ham, salami, canned tuna or salmon

1 unlidded browning dish

Preheat the browning dish for 3 minutes (or half the time recommended by the manufacturer).

Immediately place the buttered side of one of the bread slices on to the hot dish, pressing it down well with a fish slice. Cook, without covering, on Full Power for 30 seconds, then remove from the dish and place on a piece of kitchen paper.

Without wiping out reheat the dish on Full Power for 30 seconds, then cook on Full Power the remaining bread slice, buttered-side down, for 30 seconds. Leave this slice in the dish and place the filling on top of the bread, making sure that it does not lap over the sides. Cover lightly with the remaining slice, toasted side uppermost. Cook, without covering, on Full Power for 30–45 seconds or until the filling is hot. If the top is not crisp just flip the sandwich over into a previously uncovered part of the dish. There should be no need for further cooking.

In the unlikely event of a failure (i.e. the bread simply does not become crisp), all you need to do is reheat the browning dish for 30–45 seconds and then, without further microwaving, replace the sandwich on the hot surface and immediately turn it over to crisp the other side. These instructions may seem complicated but they should ensure success. You must be aware of all the pitfalls.

TRADITIONAL BREAD SAUCE

This microwave method is an adaptation of the traditional bread sauce recipe in which whole herbs and spices are infused in hot milk.

150 ml (¼ pint) milk
Small slice onion
1 blade mace
1 bay leaf
1 clove
2 peppercorns
35 g (1¼ oz) fresh white breadcrumbs
Salt
Small knob of butter

0.55 litre (1 pint) jug
1 litre (1¾ pint) bowl

Put the milk, onion, mace, bay leaf, clove and peppercorns into an 0.55 litre (1 pint) jug and cook, without covering, on Full Power for about 1 minute until the milk is steaming but not boiling. Cover and set aside for 30 minutes.

Strain the milk into a 1 litre (1¾ pint) bowl and stir in the breadcrumbs and salt. Cook, without covering, on Full Power for 1 minute, then stir in the butter before using.

Index of Recipes

One asterisk indicates a quick main-course dish,
two asterisks moderately quick